Editori

The next year will be crucial to the arts funding. For too long literature has been a support activity for other art forms instead of as important in its own right. Literature currently receives only 4% of SAC budget. After all, authors/editors need only a suitably dusty garret! In fact, of all art forms, literature has been the most consistently outstanding over centuries. This small country of ours, through its *literature* has altered the intellectual map of Europe, if not the world, irreversibly!

What follows is the response to the Cultural Commission Report from the Literature Forum for Scotland, on which I represent the magazines:

> This is a report of substance. We welcome its emphasis on participation for all of our citizens, on education, on national and international excellence, on the centrality of the languages of Scotland, on the wide role of literature in delivering these things, and the need for new investment.
>
> We are disappointed that that there is no clear recommendation for a sectoral structure that will enable literature to deliver these benefits in its own right. However, we look forward to working in a constructive framework along with the Scottish Arts Council Literature Department and The Scottish Executive to achieve the correct dynamic for literature within the reformed structures."

There is a pervading atmosphere of demoralisation among the literary magazines; we feel under threat. While we wish *The Scottish Review of Books* well, it is a *review*, not a magazine devoted to publishing new creative work. The increasing demand for professionalism, and *Chapman's* sheer longevity has increased the workload, and with it running costs, exponentially. Our grant has not significantly risen in *ten* years!

I recently acquired the following *bon mots* about why magazines matter! In *The Best of McSweeney's Vol II* Dave Eggers writes:

> Each of these journals [American lit mags] has a readership, and while that readership usually falls between 100 readers and 50,000 readers, the average readership of one of these journals is 1500. This is small by some standards, but either way is more persons than you could fit in your home. And any number of readers who would not fit in your home constitutes, we at McSweeney's think, a good number of readers ...
>
> Each magazine has a small-town feel, and a small town's worth of readers. And each of these becomes the perfect incubator for new voices; herein writers can experiment with style and voice and form, using the short-fiction form, which is forgiving of reader and writer alike.
>
> Thus here it is: you must love the short story and start your own many literary quarterlies, lest we bomb you and your people and invade your shores, and send mercenaries to fight your insurgents. To our friends we will call it a crusade. To the rest of the world we will call it liberation.

And liberation it is. Embedded in creative thinking is the severing of all the chains that bind us, and a way forward into a better future. No matter if, as is often the case with authors like James Kelman, the sky seems irredeemably dark, but that darkness is a prelude to future light. Those who devote themselves to the art of writing/editing (and editing *is* an art, and a complex one) do so because we believe in a better future for everyone. I've recently investigated funding for literary magazines in the UK, and while 10 years ago Scotland was more enlightened than other UK countries, now we abjectly lag behind. They assume we're so committed to what we do, that we'll do it anyway. You can't sacrifice yourself to 'the cause' forever. Sooner or later, you've just got to give yourself the space to stand on a beach at sunset, and enjoy.

And so, despite a detailed submission from SLAM (Scottish Literary and Arts Magazine) no mention whatsoever was made in the Cultural Commission Report even of the existence, far less anything else, of literary magazines. This is a very serious omission, and we will do what we can to draw the magazines to the attention of the powers that be.

We may be a nuisance. That is our role. This editor, for one, is committed to continuing to be so. I know how much publication in *Chapman* has meant to the authors we've published. Not all are grateful, but that's the game too. Why expect it? You do it because *it is needed!*

So, wake up Scotland! My main reason for arguing for devolution/ autonomy was that the arts in Scotland stood a better snowball's chance given a Scottish establishment. Some areas have benefitted. I've worked for a Scottish National Theatre and much else. That's going to happen now. High profile. Sponsors in best suits at the opening and all that. But what about LITERATURE. What about the *magazines?*

As far as I can gather, Scotland now is in the unenviable position of caring for its literary magazines in a way which is in fact worse than *every* other country in Europe. Plunged from half way up the scale right to the very bottom. Magazines used at least to have a perception that they mattered, and that, faults on our heads and all that, there was a healthy magazine 'scene' here. That is gone now – perception shattered. All UK countries do better than we do, and all European ones to my knowledge too. And the cost to make it all *possible* – a mere pittance!

The sheer creativity of *Chapman* and the authors we publish is amply evident here. Each contribution involves complex work with the author, to get the text to its best presentation. We have winners of the Robert Louis Stevenson Award: Donal McLaughlin, Gavin Bowd and Louise Welsh, Rab Wilson's marvellously lively translation of Horace's *Satires* into Scots, Lee Koffman on writing in a foreign language, and artist Sheila Mullen's magical landscapes and renderings of ballads – and much else. The relationships forged in the process are very special.

What was devolution *for* if not to 'liberate' the voices of Scotland? At genuine ground level, the magazines provide that voice. We are the seed-bed of tomorrow's renaissance. Give us some water!

Edwin Morgan

Acknowledge the Unacknowledged Legislators!

Go on, squawk at the font, you chubby Scotty.
You have a long song ahead of you, do you know that?
Of course not, but you let the ghost of a chuckle
Emerge and flicker as if you had thrown
Your very first chuckie and the water was playful.
It will be, and gurly too, and full of dread
Once you are grown and reckoning ahead.

So squeal a little, kick a little, what's a few drops
On that truly enormous human brow.
Man is *chelovek*, the Russians say,
The one with a forehead, the one with forethought,
The one whose mumbling and chuntering will not do,
Who knows it will not do, who lolls or bounces
Half-formed but strains for form, to be a child
And not a bundle! The bungler, the mumbler
Takes the deepest breath we are allowed,
Whistles the horizon's dawn right down
Across the book of earth, audits the figures,
Tongue and teeth and lips in line, near-perfect,
Ye see yon birkie ca'd a lord, the poet
Has hooked one leg over his simple chair-arm,
Sometimes tapping the beat upon his snuff-box,
Sometimes singing an old and well-loved air
To startlingly original effect.
He'll print it too! Won't it be in a book?
An open mind is proper in this case.
It's only poetry, after all, Someone –
I can't remember thousands of scribbling names –
Has said "Poetry makes nothing happen."
I find that slightly fundamentalist.
Yes, but do I go along with it?
I do not go along with it. No, I don't.
Do I protest too much? Probably!

Think of what I said about the child.
He is a man now, let us talk to him.
Ask him how far he thinks his *birkie*
Registers on a Richter scale of insult.
He's dead? Well, get a good dictionary.
Talk's the thing. Dialogue's the thing.

If any parliamentarian should be so remiss
As to think writers are interchangeable,
Or stupid, or irrelevant, or poor doomy creatures,
Punishments may have to be devised,
I say *may*, we want to persuade, not scold.
What is it but language that clamps
A country to glory? Ikons, concertos,
Pietàs, gamelans, gondolas, didgeridoos
Luboks, a brace of well-tuned sleigh-bells –
These are very fine, of course they are.
But better still, always far better still
Is the sparkling articulacy of the word,
The scrubbed round table where poet and legislator
Are plugged in to the future of the race,
Guardians of whatever is the case.

Notes for a Manifesto
Carl MacDougall

Are we the only people in Europe who need to be educated about ourselves? Nothing about us is good enough. Our language has been consistently undermined and denigrated and our literature is not considered suitable or distinguished enough to be taught in our schools, despite the fact that in Robert Burns we have the world's most celebrated poet.

Burns begins a litany which is as depressing as it is familiar. James Hogg's *Confessions of a Justified Sinner* is a masterwork of world literature. Walter Scott invented both the historical and romantic novels. Conan Doyle gave the world its most famous detective. Robert Louis Stevenson invented the psychological novel. Hugh MacDiarmid was considered one of the greatest European writers of the 20th century, and for more than 10 years before his death in 1978, two of Europe's leading writers were native Scots, living in Scotland – MacDiarmid and Sorley MacLean. And Muriel Spark is surely a candidate for the Nobel laureatship.

Liz Lochhead has properly instructed us that Anon was a great woman writer, and according to Edwin Muir – the ballads, the nearest we have to a specific female form, contain the greatest poetry Scotland has produced: "They bring us back again to the Scottish people and its part in the making of Scotland," he said, "for it was the people who created these magnificent poems. The greatest poetry of most countries has been written by the educated middle and upper classes; the greatest poetry of Scotland has come from the people." Muir's continual reference to the ballads as poetry presupposes he hadn't heard them sung, or that he considered tunes unimportant.

Firstly, we should stop giving prizes for Burns recitation, then tell the weans to speak properly, or to call it slang when they use the words they were rewarded for saying so well.

Artists want people to see their works and musicians enjoy playing to an audience. Writers would like to be read. We should therefore make what they write as easily accessible as possible – and not just for the benefit of the writers.

The present thinking implies that since reading standards have fallen it is a pointless waste of money sending books by Scottish writers or books about Scottish writers into Scottish schools. The fact that our present generation of writers grew up without exposure to the work of any Scottish writer and it has done them no harm should also be denied.

Books by Scottish writers should be in every Scottish primary and secondary school. We not only need books by dead Scottish writers, male Scottish writers, women Scottish writers, middle class Scottish writers or even the muddled crass Scottish writers, we need the works of living Scottish writers to be made available so that pupils can make informed choices, based on understanding rather than hope. Again, not just for the writers' benefit.

We have a language which for more than 250 years has been disparaged by the people who speak it, yet its literature is internationally distinguished. And now supernational forces threaten our voice because language is the last stand against globalisation. Spoken and written Scots has miraculously withstood a cultural onslaught from generations of school teachers, but may not survive this present global onslaught. Globalisation cannot deal with differences, it cannot tolerate a separate identity and, as the folk of Catalan and Norway can testify, language is a potent tool of resistance.

This is because it is a collective thing, capable of being shaped to an individual's needs while retaining its communicative value and relevance to the place where it originated; which, in a sense, defines the act of writing itself.

But the real reason for using our own voice and for promoting literature which uses a variety of these voices, is not that it should articulate everything, but that it can articulate things which cannot be articulated in English, or in any other language, that it articulates its own meanings, which are often beyond translation. *Glaikit* doesn't just mean stupid, *thrawn* does not mean stubborn, nor does *scunner* simply express disgust, and *driech* certainly does not mean dull.

Language groupings are no longer national, even for those of us who write with a Scots accent. Language's function is being redefined and it is possible that in the future societies will be formed to preserve language which is non-national and non-family based, such as gangsta rap and management speak. Mission statements, sound bites, blue-sky thinking and even smart objectives are under threat because of their ubiquity.

Which could mean a closer relationship with English, which has been happening in literature for quite some time. Most Scottish writers I know are at least bilingual, and the lesson of the Scots accent is that writers often mirror earlier developments, for, as we know, the ability for people to renew their spoken language is astonishingly creative.

No less an authority than the former editor of *Scottish National Dictionary* tells us the Eskimo or Inuit peoples have more than 50 names for snow. Consider then the following list of Scots words, in common everyday usage:

Wastit, swacked, fozie, miraculous, craftie, hertie, blootered, lummed-up, tosie, stotious, roarin, tovie, steamin, chippit, sappie, wambled, bleezin, soopie, washed, blebbern, roarie, mappie, cornreezie, smeikit, stavin, styterin, fankled, molassed, troosert, drucken, moidert, bladdert, drouthie, manky, bleezin, bellowsed, fuddled, stotin, slochened, mingin, swittlin, meisled, fleein, fankled, pished, minced, poopin, boggin, blin, paloovious, legless, blitzed, niddle-noddled, jakie'd guttered, capernoitit, fittered, galraviched - fu!!

There are, you will notice, more than 50 words here recorded, and there are many others I could mention, *mashed, rubber-leggit* and *wreckt* spring to mind, nor have I even considered the lexicon of phrases in everyday parlance, such as *Daein the stiff-leggit walk*, or *Waltzin the alkie two-step*, a variety of words and phrases which not only describe the condition, but states of that condition.

How can a language with such precision be useless? And it can describe a lot more. Wouldn't it be good if we could find 50 words for success or more than 50 ways of raising the profile of an under-used and underdeveloped resource, our national literary talent?

The first duty of this or any other committee should be to help Scottish children to be comfortable using and developing their own confident voice, and to give them the understanding that where a Scottish accent or dialect is concerned there is neither left nor right nor wrong.

And there is no more direct route towards achieving this than by raising and in some cases restoring their birthright, which is the raw material that is and has been the legacy of every Scottish writer.

Editor's Note: Both Edwin Morgan's poem, 'Acknowledge the Unacknowledged Legislators' and Carl MacDougall's Manifesto *were written for and read at the inaugural meeting of The Scottish Parliament Cross Party Group for Literature on 7 June this year. The enthusiasm and people's anxiety to bring about and participate change in the literary climate was indicated by the fact that about 100 people turned up. The group was created by and will be chaired by playwright and MSP Chris Ballance. We hope fervently that the work of this group will make a real difference to the status of the work of the literary community, and its funding base.*

Life Among the Ghosts of Château IKEA
Gavin Bowd

At the end of 2003, as co-recipient of the Robert Louis Stevenson Award, I spent two months in the Hôtel Chevillon. Once a rather bohemian *auberge*, frequented, at the end of the 19th century, by the likes of RLS, the *survolté* playwright and alchemist August Strindberg and Swedish artists such as Carl Larsson, it is now in safe, social-democratic hands. Imagine Proust on the outside, IKEA on the inside.

Grez-sur-Loing is an image-inducing village, between Fontainebleau and Nemours, in the midst of a great forest haunted by invisible yet noisy wild boar. The local *tabac* was well-stocked with such learned journals as *French Huntsman* and *Hooves*. The area was also in the grip of a mild psychosis: many signs forbade *les nomades*, especially Roms; the hapless *police municipale* surveilled vodka-swilling, quadbike-riding *bandes de jeunes*, who complained that there was 'nothing to do'. The mayor's brand new recycling point was burnt down on the eve of my arrival in the village: a pagan welcome? I made it to the Hôtel in a taxi driven by one Monsieur Baruta, who claimed to be descended from a depraved Polish count, a sort of Silesian de Sade.

"It is not every day you are given a lift by the Devil!"

"*Merci.*"

I shared this beautiful, yet troubled, refuge with various characters: the Arctic Circle's answer to Germaine Greer, a journalist and translator of Simone de Beauvoir and Catherine Millet; Malmo's answer to Nick Hornby, who wrote in dialect about football and whose first, unwise, question was: "Do you support Celtic or Rangers?"; and an eminent Finnish painter who was inspired when, as a child evacuee during the Continuation War against the Soviets in 41-44, his train passed through a burning station – "it was very beautiful" – and once, in the seventies, "to make ends meet", had starred, with a famous actress of the Helsinki National Theatre, in a pornographic version of *Love Story*. Meet the team.

I finished a first draft of a fictional biography of Michael Scot, *The Book of Might*, drawing on research trips to Andalusia, Sicily and the Borders. I focussed on the ambivalent relationship between Europe and Islam, embodied by the turbanned Maister, translating Aristotle and Averroes in Toledo, then advising the Emperor Frederick in Palermo and on the 'diplomatic' crusade to Jerusalem. What I wrote was imbued with the on-going conflict in Mesopotamia. I returned from the forest one fine Sunday morning to learn that a fallen dictator had been caught in his hole.

Grez captured my attention and drew my fingers to the keyboard: the mist on the canal, the heavy silence in the bare branches of the forest, hanging with the mistletoe, punctuated by gunshots, the roaring *route nationale*, the posters for missing persons, the primordial fear of lurking vagabonds. No, a dormitory village seldom sleeps soundly.

The Book of Might (extract)
Gavin Bowd

On a drunken morning, they set off. The goat and the gazelle. The garlic and the sapphire. They left the Dead Sea and climbed towards the heights. Paths wound up past dry boulders, through forbidding vegetation. Colonies of Christians and Jews were left far behind to their particular agitations. The call of minarets, too, faded into a receding valley.

"What is good and beautiful should belong to us!" said the Emperor.

The best Saracens clambered nimbly into a thinning air. Eventually, the Vulture's Nest came into view. Its barbaric solitude conferred on it a strange virginity. It was clothed in terrible yarns. No-one had had that marvellous body.

The first arrows and insults arrived. The first Moorish mountaineers made the ultimate sacrifice.

"Death to the Assassins!"

Limbs scaled the rock. Some fell inert, or fell wriggling into the hazy abyss. But others continued the climb. Arrows embedded themselves on shields, or pinged off the stone.

The Emperor and the Master remained intelligently out of range.

"No-one has ever done this before," said Frederick, who peered down at Palestine, then back up at the perverse redoubt.

"Elegance, science and violence!"

Deadly oil and shot poured from every orifice of the fort. But a grappling hook got a grip on the rampart, and children of the Atlas Mountains made their entry. The Assassins would pay a mighty price for such exertions and losses. Certainly, as of legend, they fought possessed by demons and drugs. But soon they would be garnishing the courtyard and the sinister warren of corridors and rooms. The gates were captured. The enemy only left the walls as gushing bright detritus. The Assassins had been so fearsome. Now they were so dead. They had been cut off and killed.

The Emperor and the Master were ushered into the Vulture's Nest. They watched and listened as operations were brought to a spectacular and satisfactory conclusion. Hohenzollern nostrils scoured the air. They were joined in their twitching by high altitude flies.

"It's strange. But I cannot smell much terror here."

Instead, despite all the blood, there still wafted the odour of potent herbs and other, unfamiliar, substances.

"You wonder, don't you, if such fiends believed in eternity!"

Nothing now stirred except brazen insects.

"Have you found it yet?"

The captain nodded. They were ushered into the study. It was stuffed with books, tarot cards and other potent symbols.

"And, Your Majesty, we found this man hiding in a hole."

Frederick went up to the high priest, slapped his grim and grimy face and tugged hard at his bushy black beard. He turned to the men under his command:

"You know what to do. The magic rack!"

And so they set to work, with manipulations of the body that explored the laws of geometry, gravity and obscenity, and that soon had this Assassin squealing the truth. The secret door was found, the code successfully entered. The occupiers strode into a treasure trove of astrolabes and alembics, jars of the rarest substances, some filled with exotic and extinct species, or imaginatively monstrous human and animal foetuses. An archer looked slightly sad. The Emperor ruffled his Bohemian curls:

"It began with the laughter of children. It will end with it, I assure you."

Indeed, they had uncovered a massive array. There was so much material for transmutation and transcendence.

"You see, Master Michael, I have kept my mad promise."

Michael admired this armoury, although such a triumph seemed to diminish his own might.

The men began to lovingly strip the Vulture's Nest. Nothing of any value would be left behind. Frederick plunged his face into a smouldering bowl of hashish, gasped with pleasure, then made for the exit, tugging at the leash around the neck of the broken high priest.

"What begins with disgust ends in a stampede of perfumes!"

The Master perked up and enjoined:

"What begins in all loutishness ends with angels of fire and of ice!"

August Philippe

The stone had been very cold but very dry. He had scaled it like he had learned at the Avertical Club, the one created by the mayor. His feet and hands found holds in arrow slits now colonized by pigeons. With each new triumph over gravity and common sense, there was an indignant grey clatter. He would only look down when he reached the top.

From the Tour de Ganne, there was an excellent view. First the medieval garden, then the famous bridge. Beneath it passed the river Loing, inhabited by wisps of mist and ravenous factions of ducks and geese. Then the brown, bare forest, infested with shy and succulent boar.

He thought of those Sunday mornings of authorised hunting. Or the hot summer nights when you sat, drank and waited for the wild to appear. Then the eloquent hours when you recounted what or whom you had 'done'. The municipal police-car had drawn up at the end of the bridge. The fat old man had got out, and was shouting:

"Philippe, get down from there."

Philippe feigned to drop from the ruined tower. A full thirty metres.

The young man laughed.

The Tour de Ganne was an august ruin. Its heart was blasted open like an unfortunate partridge. Those walls had incarcerated Blanche de Castille and Robert Le Bon. But the dungeons were no more. The Hundred Years War had ended centuries ago. France and England now jousted at sport, on television. And the fair Louise de Savoie had long since expired from plague.

"Get down from there!"

The policeman preferred shooing on travellers.

Philippe looked towards the playing fields and the camp-site. He remembered the Swedish girls they had met by the crêperie. There had been some sultry, sweaty hours in that caravan. Then he looked towards the burnt-out recycling place, created by the mayor. For a while, those flames had warmed the boys and girls of Grez. Though the melting plastic brought tears to the eyes.

The day before, he had seen a barge pass on the canal. It had been called *Le Bon vivant*. The green plastic dancefloor had been empty save for shrubs and urns. Philippe had waved to the helmsman, without reciprocation. The barge chugged away into the mist, towards a town and strong demand for festivity. He had walked back to the village.

The municipal policeman was gesticulating. He was standing where the gang would normally meet and take turns to sit in the souped up Citroen, throbbing with techno. Or they would take one of the mopeds and race the circuit. Grez. Moncourt. Montigny. Bourron-Marlotte. Back to Grez and the deepening dark and chill of winter.

"Get down from there!"

Was he going to call the police?

"I will not tell your parents!"

"Oh them?" shouted Philippe.

The words hung as vapour then disappeared.

Over the wall of the Hôtel Chevillon, he could see an artist. With her long red hair, she must have been Swedish. She was painting the river and the trees before the campsite. She had been there every day for weeks, capturing the varying light.

He turned and stared downwards. The milestone stamped with a fleur-de-lys. Philippe-Auguste had lived here before leaving to become King.

"Please come down from there!"

La Marina

There was a trace of blood in the *escalope milanaise*. A pinkish leak from the battered white flesh.

Outside *La Marina*, cars and articulated lorries flowed down the *route nationale*. The drivers were blacked out. All you could see were pairs of lights, white or yellow, that peered into the desperate brightness of the restaurant, then left, probably forever.

I had come from the forest. I had passed the house bedecked with Christmas lights and effigies of Santa Claus and snowmen. It was still only November, and an insipid drizzle fell on the Gâtonnais. The owners of that weird house had only just taken down their Hallowe'en horrors.

"Papa Noël!" shouted the youngest daughter. The owner told her to shut up. "Papa Noël!"

She wanted a gift. I stabbed my fork, cut with my knife. I noticed the nick on the back of my hand.

I had come out of the forest and taken the subway. I had passed the psychotic Alsatian. 'Je monte la garde!' said the sign outside its fenced and shuttered home. Could the canine also read and write? I had followed the traffic's floodlights. I had meticulously rubbed my soles at the entrance.

On the solitary lamp-post, I had seen the poster. Estelle of Guermantes was still missing. Judges and jurors were converging on the village for a re-enactment. They felt it could bring them nearer the truth. I put the last bit of escalope in my mouth. I sipped the house red wine. And I remembered the girl's sweet little face, her body's stammering announcement of puberty.

"That man should be strung up!" said the father at the next table.

It was the only other table occupied. He was enunciating on justice to his patient family. His eldest daughter's eyes caught mine then scurried into the undergrowth of a laminated menu. The subject of conversation turned to the proposed rise in the tax on tobacco.

"Papa Noël!" She still wanted a gift. The little girl was finally ushered to a back-room. They would lock her in with the dog.

Parts of the body could become detached, irrevocably. I thought of the eyelashes that had begun to drop onto my pillow during the night.

It was the eldest daughter who took my empty plate. God, she had changed. All the villagers thought that. The fine, provocative curves, the big-lashed, brown eyes. The owners of *La Marina* were genuinely Italian. You heard them muttering in dialect at the back. Perhaps they had left a sun-kissed harbour, crowded with yachts.

The girl looked at me. There was no trace of a smile. She just lifted my plate and my knife and fork, and walked away, with an order for dessert and my eyes travelling over her abdomen. She retreated behind a false marble arch.

The traffic flowed past *La Marina*. Northwards and southwards. Lovers and merchandise would wake up in different countries. You might rub your eyes, carefully. I had to quit *La Marina* for the great forest.

The tiramisu was far too cold. Its heart was as chilled and unpalatable as a morgue. I finished the red wine, and wiped my lips on the paper napkin. There was a red and muddy smear.

That girl was looking at me with her big-lashed eyes. I smiled a dazzling smile. She remained beautiful and dour. That did not bother me. I wanted her to know that I knew that bills have to paid.

The Palace

"When Henri IV decided to make Fontainebleau his residence, he expelled the convent."

The guide seemed impressed by such royal fiat. Friedrich imagined the generations of benighted women, scuttling from the grounds with their few possessions and wounded faith. Axel was looking out onto the Cour des Adieux. He imagined Napoleon addressing his last troops, whipped by the Prussians and the Brits, before deportation to St Helena.

Someone had said:

"You have the right to kill your Emperor!"

They did not even have the courage to do that.

The two men were shown the cramped and musty splendour of the theatre. The neat rows of seats were now covered with dirty linen. The guide lifted one of the sheets:

"The seat of the Second Emperor."

Axel and Friedrich took turns to sit and survey the stage, and laughed at the memory of that fat backside which got a right good kicking at Sedan. Then the guide attracted their attention to grills that lined the gods.

"Through those grills, the police could survey the entire audience. Even the actors."

They nodded, politely.

Tacked boots tapped on the varnished but creaking floorboards. They continued through the gilded monotony of the Palace.

"What a boring house!" exclaimed Axel. "Never-ending pomposity."

No corner was spared a desperation to please.

They were shown a bath.

"Every time someone washed, they placed a cloth. When they had finished, the cloth was removed, and replaced by another. In this way, water, which was very precious, could be conserved."

The two officers smiled and thought of the shortages. The Marshal was saying that poverty was penance, that the nation would regain its original features. His people had nothing to lose but their jowls.

"And look at this stucco. It is not real. It is only painted like stucco. As is this mahogany. And this marble. There is no marble to be found in France."

Axel looked at the guide: the darned clothes, the cheaply oiled hair, the drooping belt.

"He would take a *wurst* for a *saucisse*!"

The guide wondered why the blond boy was suddenly smiling.

The tour moved on. The Frenchman waxed lyrical at the red heels of Louis XV. Friedrich sneered as he was shown the discreet entrances for cooking staff. Hadn't an intelligent Jew once talked about the suppression of the reality of labour? Then they yawned as they were shown around the gifts from an Emperor of China. The oriental kitsch glowed dimly in the candlelight. There was little power left in this country.

The guide had disappeared, lost in a monologue about faded and failed frescoes. The two young soldiers stopped in a gallery.

Pris au piège

A wolf was caught in a man-trap. Its leg was horribly broken. The smashed femur pierced the skin. To the doomed and desperate animal clung the fangs and claws of servile hounds.

"Barbaric!" barked Axel.

Friedrich nodded then pointed to another tableau.

Tête de cerf bizarre

Just an antler, ripped from a noble head. Rough strands of bloody flesh still clung to it.

"Deviant," said Axel.

The way the still life sat, it looked like a Picasso.

The guide wanted them to see the last chapel, even inspect the grounds' elaborate system of waterways. But they dug in their shiny boots, and looked out of the window.

The flames were finishing their dinner. The synagogue had been almost completely burned to the ground. A soldier was shooing away onlookers. A couple of firemen, far too late and half-hearted, were throwing precious water on the ashes. The guide had forgotten Rossetto:

"There was an explosion here two nights ago."

He looked both flustered and elated. Axel noticed the fleur-de-lys pinned to his lapel.

"I guess that such things happen a lot in your great country."

The young men said nothing, and took the nearest exit. They descended the grand, grey and hideous stairway. Above them was draped a huge swastika flag. How its red eclipsed the pale brick of the Palace!

Their boots tapped-tapped to the Cour des Adieux. Their thoughts were with the lads, and the lightning march into Russia.

Persephone Pit-stop

At the grotto, the cars sped into the chicane, then continued their screaming around the Lago di Pergusa. Another lap. She watched from the terrasse of the Hotel Déméter. Still she could not see her. She had not for a long time.

Once she had seen pink flamingos on the lake. They were on their way to a winter in North Africa. White egrets. Wild geese. They slid into that smooth, unfathomable water. Then they disappeared.

The whole earth seemed to tremble with the relentless racing of the cars. The men out there were going at full throttle. Their lives depended on it. She put her palms up to her ears. It was no use. She dropped her hands. Between two fingers was a strand of grey hair. Another lap.

She sipped the cocktail. Her hand trembled. She spilled some of the garish liquid on her blouse. Then she stared beyond the wire fence and the race track to the reeds. She imagined her rising from that water, dripping, resplendent, in that young and fateful beauty.

The leading car, red as hell, dashed the image. She looked for the face of the driver, but it was masked by a helmet and velocity. He would soon growl at the Casa di Principessa.

Around and in this lake, there would always be a porcupine, a white owl and a frog. A tortoise would always lumber around its banks.

From the Hotel Demeter, she had seen the lake's metamorphoses. Pink. Green. Blue. But always still, only seasonally ruffled by migratory birds. At night, it was a black mirror for the stars and planets.

The winner now charged towards the checkered flag. At the *tribuna* men with concealed penises and pasts gripped the railing, or gesticulated. The police had their eyes peeled on the *autodromo*.

A man had won. The other cars whined to their irrelevant conclusions.

She often thought of scaling that fence, then walking calmly over the tarmac. If she made it she would walk into the water. She would see how deep it was. She might find her there, among the weed, fish and frogs.

She could not, and returned to her winter.

Illuminations

for Anne Armagnac

You phoned to say
Paris is grey
not gay

The city sulked on the edge
of an anti-cyclone
a grey lid weighed
on Le Rendez-vous des amis

You spoke of carpets
swarming with new-born
a Sunday spent walking
in a beautiful wood

When you are young and alone
you have to fill
the void in front of you

Cold calm air
welcomed the season
a harp enriched
my capital vista

*We read so much less
than during the war*

I would descend upon
the unlit city
through mobile voices
and smiles to no-one

An immigrant asked
*Do you know the cause
of vertigo?*

Stores struggled to sell
the Nativity
Blizzards in the south
had marred the launch
of a magic book   *Sacré-Coeur*

Still Air

walking back from the market
a white bag full of
bread and wine

still air
on birch bark
boar and gunshots
had dissolved

a simple bonjour
a smiling girl
kept her spaniel
to the path

white bodywork
battered and peeling
a rolled-down window

*Can you show me the place
where I went to fish
as a child?
The river had two branches.
There was an island.*

We became three holes
filled with still air.
We moved like mist
on dammed waters. *Grez-sur-Loing*

Avenue

Duck couples beneath sphinxes
with broken noses.
A municipal wind
is blowing in the leaves.

A blue bird in bare branches
marching to the château.
A winter tourist a memory
of having you. *Fontainebleau*

Detail

Venus had crossed the sun,
but we did not notice.
Our train just slid
through the Valley of Flowers.

A young mother in red
raised her child towards us.
Their eyes painted the window,
an enlightenment picture.

Our thoughts flickered
as lightning on the orchards.
We were butterflies pinned
in museum twilight.

The mountains rained
on Sophocles Street.
Our doormat said:
Today is a good day. *Hermannstadt*

Clothes Lines

The clothes that were worn
Now hang on the line,

Guard moisture from the ground
And cede it to the wind.

Maybe mother would gather them
And bring them from the garden,

Smelling of rain and smoke,
Touched by leaves and twigs.

Tomorrow bodies will wear them,
Work and sweat for weeks,

Lie hoping for the cleansing
Found between open thighs.

Reconstruction

On scaffolding,
pigeons make the sound
of human lovers.

At times, their wings
burst from old brick,
like a thumb flicks
the pages of a book.

Gavin Bowd

Profiles
Stephen Sharp

The Vet

He folded the cat's skin between his fingers. He vaccinated the puss against flu. The vaccine would "engender protection for a year. Guaranteed". It would definitely be a good idea, however, to have an expensive 'booster' in 12 months' time.

The Late Russian President

Moscow Radio instructed the world in English that all of "progressive humanity" should go into mourning and remember the President. The news was delayed in Albania. A British statesman recalled how the president thumped the table if he did not get his way. However, in comparison with Soviet generals he was a moderate.

The leader had been ill for years. In the hours before his death, Russian newsreaders put on black suits and solemn music was played. From this, foreign journalists inferred that a senior politician had died. The President had long been tipped for the grave by Kremlin watchers.

British news reporters were rather tolerant of the expansion of the USSR during his presidency. A dissident said that he disliked the Soviet system but he had nothing against the late leader personally. He disliked the system but not the people. But can one distinguish a system from the people who keep it going? The dissident said that he did not blame the President in person for the invasion of Czechoslovakia. It was caused by the laws of history, not by the work of one man. An American reporter put the opposite view: that individuals and not the laws of history were responsible for invasions and wars. Therefore it mattered whether a moderate or a hard-liner got the succession.

The Spy

John was questioned by the police about sexual assaults on young children. After the police released him, he confessed to his wife. Not only had he abused children but he had also been a Russian spy. He told the police he was a paedophile. His wife told the police that John had been a spy.

John was recruited by the Soviets while with the RAF in Berlin. He said his personality disorder had caused him to admire the Russian system. Many Soviet dissidents were imprisoned for personality disorders. John worked for GCHQ in Cheltenham, where he analysed decoded messages. He would tell the Russians which codes the British had cracked. The Russians then provided the British with inaccurate intelligence.

In 1977 John became a taxi-driver.

The judge listened to the evidence against John in private because it was secret. He told John he would go to prison for 38 years. The Spy said that after his release he would try to atone for his espionage.

The PM told the House of Commons that John had worked alone. Twice John had been "Positively vetted". A former Foreign Secretary asserted that the positive vetting system had failed and therefore that British agents should spy on each other. The PM disagreed since this would increase the number of people knowing British secrets. Why had John spied for Russia? They only paid him a few thousand pounds.

A Welsh MP affirmed he was more disgusted by John's sexual crimes than by his spying. A socialist said that as the Government was short of money it should auction British secrets. The Chief Secretary to the Treasury pretended to make a note of this suggestion.

The New Russian Leader
Dimitri was once in command of the KGB. It was claimed that he was "personally" responsible for the invasion of Hungary in 1956. A Kremlinologist claimed that history was more complicated than this, and that the invasion of Hungary was inevitable.

Dimitri spoke English and was regarded as an intellectual. Kremlinologists said he was a hard liner. He was chairman of a committee overseeing the funeral of his predecessor. The news came to a synthesis of views on 1956: Dimitri was not totally responsible for the invasion but he was partly responsible. Then it was disclosed he was ambassador in Hungary in '56 and had held a 'Judas Supper' for leaders of the uprising.

The Comic Intellectual
He asserted that Sir F Laker was a travel agent. Wouldn't it be funny if Sir F went bankrupt again?

The Female Professional
Geraldine claimed she had read all the news reports on the spy who loved children but she could not understand what 'Positive vetting' was. She thought there should be greater parliamentary control of the secret service. Geraldine would like her MP to know what was going on. The MP must find out what the government meant by 'positive vetting?' He could store the definition vicariously on her behalf.

As a working mother, she believed teenage children could run a house on their own. The role of mother was now superfluous. Geraldine disagreed with middle-aged ladies who believed they were the only ones who could do the shopping. Men were capable of doing the cooking.

Geraldine asserted that police officers, male police officers, were racially prejudiced. Crime had causes such as unemployment, which exonerated the poor who shoplifted. Giving the police more power would not decrease the crime rate. Society once attributed to women the qualities it now ascribed to racial minorities.

Geraldine was once a nun. She thought the ideas about sex of the Catholic Church were mistaken. The dogma that birth control was wrong she rejected. This was not an eternal truth. Birth control was once morally wrong but is no longer immoral because the world is over-populated. Sex was one of few pleasures enjoyed by Brazilians. Christ should have let Mary Magdalene touch him after the resurrection. While criticising the Messiah, she held her hands on her chest, as if in prayer.

William –The Trade Unionist
The Pension funds were the wealthiest organisations in the country. They should contribute to a National Investment Bank. The Government should guarantee them a high rate of return equal to that on gilt-edged securities. The Investment bank would create jobs. The pension fund managers thought there was a conflict between maximising profits and reducing unemployment.

The number of doctors and nurses should be determined not by economics but the health of the country. Social justice should determine the wages of nurses. The government believed it could afford more nurses only if their wages were low.

Marc – The Liberal intellectual
Marc said that people who awarded prizes to perpetuate their names, such as Nobel, were slapping themselves on the back. They were being "self-congratulatory". He thought that the moral arguments against nuclear weapons were not conclusive. It might be morally correct for Britain to disarm unilaterally. The theory of nuclear deterrence might be morally wrong. Saying "ban the bomb" was simplistic. If British nuclear weapons were superfluous to the needs of NATO, then Britain should disarm. Marc held his interlocked fingers on the desk before him.

Marc conceded that the nationalised industries had been inefficient. He had once hoped that nationalisation would promote co-operation between management and the workers. His macro beliefs were Keynesian. The rate of interest was not the only variable the chancellor should manipulate. He should adjust "Real Variables." Marc was a corporatist; he believed in co-operation. It was an alternative to private or public ownership of the economy.

The drive of narrative impaired the truth of politicians' memoirs.

Marc listened to a theatre critic say that TV should be banned on Sundays and that this would prevent the British from becoming a nation of spectators. Marc looked at a woman and observed loudly, "what did you just say about clichés?" Marc and the woman had a bet on what the critic would say. The critic ignored this and spoke of his love of wine.

Marc was opposed to the devaluation of the pound. He believed in a state education system and in the freedom of parents to send their offspring to public schools. He believed in reflating the economy. The critic giggled at this left-wing cliché. Marc thought that, in contrast to Japan, Britain was inward-looking. Japan researched what Europe desired, then manufactured it in great quantities. The British showed little interest in what the Japanese wanted. He thought the media was responsible for the state of Britain. It did not present international news accurately. It showed more interest in a recent colonial war than in world trade. The critic said, "You mean the BBC".

The Comedian
He related how an impresario invited him to appear on the Royal Variety Show. He amused the mother of the Queen by telling how the impresario used to sell underwear from a barrow.

The comic was mugged on his way to the theatre. He patted his pocket to demonstrate to the mugger that he had no wallet. "Will it be OK if I write you out an IOU?" The IOU joke continued; he hadn't been able to pay the Taxi so he wrote an IOU. Then he said, "I'm not the only one here who does not carry cash."

The Sculptor
Rod believed that sculpture expressed feelings as well as represented objects. He wished to convert Munch's Scream into a non-abstract sculpture. A friend had asked of one of his early steel sculptures if it had been left by the builders. The interviewer laughed, as if he would not have made the same mistake. It was now self-evident that abstract steel sculptures were art. Rod's influences were Picasso and Henry Moore. Moore had offered him work. They co-operated in brass. Rod quoted a critic who didn't think this was art. This he could accept as a correct judgement only of his early representational work. The work of transition from representation to abstraction was steel Stonehenge.

The Newspaper Man
Dick said the price of newsprint was increasing faster than the rate of inflation so the big dailies would all make a loss this year. If the price of a tabloid increased, its circulation fell. The recession had caused a fall in advertising revenue; classified job adverts had declined in proportion to the increase in unemployment. The only way out was to cut production costs, the biggest – overmanning. A few voluntary redundancies now would avoid thousands being made redundant if their papers closed.

The Writer
Goat intended to write a novel without characters about monetarism. The preface would say that economic theory was fiction. In fact everything was fiction. Therefore it was possible to write a novel without characters. The Goat was a teacher; his subject was literature.

The Young Writer
You need to be totally in control of the sentence to surprise the reader.

The Old Writer
When Charlie was deep in a novel, the characters took possession of him. There was nothing wrong in being an entertainer, in wanting to make the reader turn the page. Charlie had led a life of the mind and hardly noticed real people.

Shanta Acharya

Dispossessed

We embarked on this pilgrimage
dreaming of placing trust
in our adopted homeland, thought
life would no longer be easily snatched;
did not reckon that death had so many paths,
so many notions of justice and redemption.

What are you after?
Our souls are sick, moving from harbour to harbour.
To know itself a soul must look into its own soul.

We knew the islands were beautiful
when we stowed ourselves, leaving the rest to God,
praying to the immortal sea to bring us here.

Our country is closed in,
        our days clouded by war.
At night fear rose like the moon
spreading its shroud over death and hunger.

We came here believing in freedom,
our history a mascot we carried in our hearts.

We did not expect a miracle;
        have we not paid enough?
If you need more   take us,
whatever is left of our dreams, our possessions;
only spare our children, our future …

Somewhere, Something

We travel not to explore another country
but to return home fresh, bearing gifts.

Our lives the airports we fly from,
our bodies and souls, maps and compasses –
        days the journeys we make,
past the continents we leave behind.

Surely there is somewhere, something
that justifies our coming and going?

Isn't that why we seek evidence from each other
of experiences worth dying for
        as we partake love in starlight
brittle with frost and the sharp taste of blood?

Let's fly free, not nailed to a mast;
    see the universe with new eyes
not blinded by shadows that light casts.

Coconut Milk

My basket was heavy with shopping,
but the coconut milk was missing.
Sainsbury did not have the ready-to-cook
variety, in a tin, made in Thailand –
creamy as full-fat milk and just as silky.

Will this do? The kind, withered shop assistant
asked, handing me a solid cake of coconut milk.
I smiled; he smiled, shuffled off, satisfied.

That evening I cook the prawns
with fine-chopped onions, mushrooms, tomatoes
stirring in slivers of the milk.

The flavours waft through wide open windows into the sunset.

Moving to the rhythm of old Hindi film songs
I savour your presence.
    The sun retires behind
trees that sway to the *raga* and *rasa* of living –

I see that like the sun, moon and stars
you are always there, though briefly revealed.
Our paths diverge, and we must let go ...
Sprinkling freshly chopped coriander leaves,
ground garlic and crushed chilli on the curry,
my eyes are blinded with grief and a child's fury.

The Last Illusion

Lying awake like the sky all night
I fall asleep with the promise of dawn
waking in a rainbow land beyond our universe
part Vegas, part Himalayas
welcomed by an unfamiliar God.

Not the gods, goddesses, saints, saviours
I had grown accustomed to –
no father, grand parents, friends or ancestors.

All believers of truth, goodness, integrity
and other such virtues despatched to earth
to pay their dues, mend lives blighted by ethics.

The gods to themselves kept Justice;
humans held on to Hope –
the strong, pure in mind and action
believing most in divine retribution.

Ushered into this transcendent realm
I encounter history's countless evil men
whose greed and pride, hypocrisy and cruelty
plunged their peers into unimaginable pain.

These were no monsters regaling me
with stories of their inhumanity.
Smiling at my shock of recognition –
the last illusion,
their bacchanalia uninterrupted by my confusion –
they invite me to join in their jamboree.

What any human knows is finite,
   what we do not know is infinite …

Angels singing carry me back gently to myself
leaving me to figure It out …
I am woken by the cold, clear light of day.

Sheila Mullen – *Blue Woods*

Rainbow Burdies

Eleanor Thomson

Look at yese, pijin-burdies, sittin on the windaysill. Look at yese ... pretty ... Ay, so y'are – dead pretty. **No! No!** *Wrang word ...*

No *dead* pretty cause dead's no a nice word ... *Dead!* **Dead – DEED – dead-deed, dead-deed** – stane cauld – just like inside the fridge ... ice cream cauld. Nae breath ... No breathin ... No speakin cause yer lips is blue wi the cauld ... Naw, it's *definitely* no a nice word ...

Ah'm huvin a wee think ... Whit ahm ur tae dae pijins?

Kin ye tell me, eh? Tell me whit ah kin dae? Ur yese tryin tae tell me? Yer wee voices is that nice but ah don-know whit yer sayin ...

Brrrreew, brrreew ... yer sayin, ... Brrreew, brrreew ...

That's a nice wee sound but ah don't speak pijin – naebdy does.

Ah dun-no – naebudy tae tell anythin tae, pijins. Whit am ur tae dae? Mammy's sleepin, pijins. She'll no wake up, so she'll no ... She must be awfy tired, pijins. D'ye know – ma Mammy told me she likes yese, pijins. Ah like ye's as well, so ah dae. Ah like tae look at aw yer wee smooth feathers ... Mibbe ye'll let me touch ye? A wee stroke wi ma fing-er?

Naw ... ? No yet ... ? Ye're gettin used tae me though, aren't ye ... ? Ye're definitely gettin used tae me. C'mon ... Ther ye are – some wee crumbs on the windaysill ... That's it ... Eat it up like a good boy.

That's whit Mammy says tae me, *Eat up yer tea like a good boy, Patrick.*

"But Mammy," ah say back tae hur, "ah'm no **like** a good boy – ah'm **ur** a good boy ... "

Then she laughs, burdies. She laughs an laughs, *Aw, son – ye'll aye be a good boy fur yer Mammy, won't ye?*

Then she says, *Ye aye get me laughin like a hyena, son.*

That means laughin really loud – like a hyena – a kinda foreign dug that's wild – it wid eat ye – ye dinnae get nae hyena dugs in Glesga, ma Mammy says, so ye dinnae need tae worry, pijins – they'll no get ye ...

... Stay up here – twenty three stories high – an they'll *definitely* no get ye. That's wan good thing aboot bein up high, pijins, in'tit? That's *definitely* good ... as well as whit ye kin see oot the windays ...

Ma Mammy says some folk would pay a big loada money fur tae see whit **we** get tae see – right ower them hills, burdies. Ye'll know them, eh? Ye'll fly ther in the summer, eh? The Campsies. They're snowy the noo fur the winter ... fur Chrismas. Chrismas's comin soon ...

Jingle bells, jingle bells ... Santa's comin tae awrah good boys n girls ...

Ye know, ma Mammy *definitely* likes yese, pijins. She keeps the fat aff the grillpan fur ye's.

Breed n drippin fur the pijins, son. Keeps them nice n warm in this cauld weather ... Oan a Saturday efter wur bacon n eggs, *feed the burdies* – breed n drippin ... Cannae be a Saturday the day, pijins, cause Mammy's no made the bacon n eggs ... She's still in her bed, so she is ...

She telt me a story aboot ye's, pijins ... *Look at aw the lovely colours on the pijins' necks,* she says, *lovely colours catchin the light. Patrick ... d'ye know how they got these beautiful shiny colours?*

Ah widnae know ... So a jist said, "Naw Mammy, ah dunno – d'*you* know Mammy?"

Well, Patrick, she says tae me. *Ther wis wance a wee boy pijin that wanted tae find oot whit wis high up above the sky – he wantit tae know if ther really wis a heaven like God says. He says tae his Mammy, "Ah'm gonny fly right up high an see whit God's like in heaven, Mammy, an come back tae tell ye."*

So the wee burdie flew an flew until he reached the gatesa heaven. When the gates opened a great big rainbow filled the sky. The wee burdy flew intae heaven but a Saint called Peter who watches the gates said he couldnae go any further until God telt him tae. The wee burdy said, "But whit ah'm a gonnae tell ma Mammy when ah get back hame? Ah promised that ah wid tell hur whit God an heaven's like!" Big Peter jist smiled an said, "She'll know ye've been tae heaven when ye fly back tae her through the rainbow." So the wee burdy flew back tae earth through the big beautiful rainbow an aw the lovely colours brushed ower his feathers. When he got back, the wee pijin hud a beautiful shiny ring o colour roun his neck – jist like the lovely colours o the rainbow an then his Mammy knew he hud been tae heaven an back. AW the wee boy pijins after him got the same ring o colour tae show that their great great great great great gran-faither hid flew through the rainbow tae heaven an back.

D'ye like that story burdies? Ah dae. Ah like it a lot, so ah dae ... Mammy's told me it millionsa times ...

Ah wish Mammy wi'd waken up, burdies. Will ah try wakenin hur? Whit ur ye's sain, wee burdies? Brrreew ... Brrreew ... 'S a nice sound that. Go an waken Mammy? Ay, OK, then ... ah will ...

... ah'm back, burdies. She's still sleepin ... Maybe she's ...

Maybe ... Oh, ah cannae think, burdies ...

Whit um ur tae dae? Ah dunno naebdy tae say tae, burdies. Mammy's sleepin too much, so she is ... Ah know she's no hungry, but, 'cause ye're no hungry when ye're sleepin ... Ah'm hungry ... Ah'm huvin a piece n jam, burdies. *You* kin huv some tae.

Mammy'll no let me touch the cooker, neither she will ... She gets angry at me if ah touch the nobs on it. Ah kin make a cuppa tea cause ah kin fill up the kettle an switch it on, so ah kin. Ah'll jist huv a wee cuppa tea wi ma piece ... That's better, burdies. Cuppa tea an a piece n jam's nice, eh? Ye kin huv some mer breed, tae ...

Ther y'are ... a wee bit breed, burdies ... Ye wantin in? In ye come if ye want ... Ther y'are ... Mammy says that tae visitors, *In ye come.* That means she's happy tae let ye intae the hoose. She might hear ye's, pijins, an waken up an say, *In ye come.* Ther's a bigger ledge inside the kitchen winday fur yese tae staun on. That's it … Eat up yer crumbs …

Ay … ye're lettin me stroke ye a wee bit noo, eh? OK, OK – no too much – don't fly away … Ye cannae go on the cooker, *naw* … cum ere! Back tae the windaysill – that's it … good burdy. Back tae yer wee pals.

Ah'm worried, burdies. Ah dun-no whit day it is … It cannae be Seterday cause Mammy's no made the bacon'n'eggs an it cannae be Monday or Thursday … She goes tae hur job on a Monday mornin n on a Thursday. She goes oot at five in the mornin – that's dead early, burd … **No!**

No! **Wrang word!** *Wrong word* … . *Don't say it.* Don't say **dead.**

That's a **bad** word … **Dead's deed, deed, deed …**

It's makin me shake, burdies. *Ah'm huvin a panic* … **Mammy! Mammy!** Deed's bad! Bad …

… *bad* … *bad* … **cannae stop** … **shakin** … *Mammy* … **MAMMY!** Bad … bad … bad …

breathe, Mammy … says – big … deep … *breaths* … that's it … that's it …

… OK … OK, burdies. OK … it's all gone now … breathin … breathin like a good boy … Ah'm OK, burdies … Ay – OK …

Ah'm sorry wee burdies – ah've made ye feart.

OCH! *AAWWW!* Look silly burdies – ye've knocked everythin doon … AW the cups is oan the fler … Mammy'll be angry, burdies. **She** doesnae get feart when ah hiv a big panic … Mammy says tae me, *Panic's ower, Patrick, panic's ower … big deep breaths … big, big breaths … that's it …*

Mammy aye puts a cauld cloot on ma neck when ah huv an attack, burdies. She's sleepin, but. She doesnae know ah've hud a panic or she wid say, *A wee cauld cloot fur tae cool ye doon, son. Ther y'are … better noo?*

She cannae put a cloot on ma neck, but. She's sleepin … She's sleepin, burdies! Sleepin too long … Who kin ah tell, burdies? Ah dun-no – dae *you*.? She must be awfy tired …

Ur ye lookin fur mer crumbs? Ye're awfy hungry wee pijins, uren't ye? Ther y'are, wee burdie. Ma wee favrite burdie wi the rainbow neck … That's it … that's right. Come ontae ma fing-ers …

Oh … That's tickly, so it is. Yer wee cauld feet and yer wee peckin beak's tickly in ma haun … Big hauns. Big man's haun … Lookit it … Ma Mammy says, *Ye've got hauns like shovels, son – a big man's hauns but ye'll never be anythin else but ma wee boy!*

Heh, burdy! *Naw, naw,* stoapit! Ye shouldnae sit oan the worktop, pijin … Come back ontae ma haun. That's it …

Here's yer wee pal comin tae get some crumbs as well …

AAWWW! Och! *Pijin jobbies on the worktop!* Ye're a **bad** pijin. **Bad … No! … don't fly away**. Don't fly aroon in the kitchen. *Ye'll hurt yersel.*

Look, ye've got feathers aw ower the place an yer *jobbies* is goin on the **walls**, noo …

Come back! Och, yer no getting any mer crumbs if ye dinnae come back! C'mere. Here … nice crumbs. Good wee burdy. Eat up. Mammy'll no be pleased wi the mess, pijins. Aw ower the fler as well, so it is …

Mammy cleans the flers at BestShops up the road oan a Monday mornin an a Thursday mornin, burdies. She tells me ah've tae stay warm in ma bed till she gets back hame then she brings me ma breakfast an ah get up tae go tae the Centre … A wee bus comes fur tae tak me ther, burdies. Ah make things at the Centre oan Mondays and Thursdays. If ah cannae go oan the wee bus tae work at the Centre ma Mammy phones them. Ah wish ah knew the number, burdies. Ah could say tae them "Whit day is it?" an they wid tell me.

Ah dun-no naebdy else. Ma Mammy's sleepin an ma Daddy's away tae heaven pijins. Mammy says God called tae him.

Ma Mammy says he's away tae heaven through the rainbow. He went when ah wis awfy wee, she says. *A wee boy, Patrick* …

Ah'm big, noo, pijins. Really big. *A **big** man*, Mammy says. She says ah'm aboot six fit wi big clumsy feet tae go wi it. *Get yer size nines affa ther*, she says tae me. That means ma feet's big an she gets annoyed when ah tramp oan things. Ah think ma feet's bigger than size nines, though …

Ma birthday's oan Chrismas day, burdies – same day as Jesus' birthday. Jesus said ye huv tae be good tae get intae heaven … Mammy says, *Life begins at forty*. Ah'm forty oan Chrismas day, so ah ah'm.

Chrismas is soon, burdies. Mammy an me wis goanny put up the decrations. Maybe we could the day if it's no Monday or Thursday. If it's Saturday or Sunday we could … but she's sleepin …

Kin ye waken her up, pijins? Mibby ye could …

Aahh've goat a good ***idea*** pijins. Mibby if she heard ye she might open her eyes … D'ye think so – d'ye think that's a good idea? Ah think it is …

C'moan then – that's it. Yer lettin me hold ye noo … That's good …

Come away in, burdies, ***come away in***. Ah'll take ye through first, ma wee favrite rainbow burdy … We'll get yer pals in a minute … Good pijin … That's it … Come an see Mammy in hur room … That's it … sit ther oan the bed, nice. Ah'm away tae get yer pals frae the kitchen …

… c'moan pijins – yer pal's through wi Mammy … Ay, ye've tae go an see ma Mammy, so ye hiv! C'moan, wee pijins. Intae ma hauns … some nice crumbs fur yese … Don't worry … Ah'm no goanny squash ye. Ah'm bein careful. Here's some mer breed – nice wee crumbs fur yese … Ay … yer lettin me hold ye noo – ye've got used tae me, eh?

Oops! Ye comin tae ride oan ma heed? Ye don't like me takin yer wee pal withoot ye, eh? Make yer nice noises – that's it – Brrrreew, brrreew … Waken Mammy up …

Mammy – *ma wee favrit rainbow burdies fur tae see ye!*

Keep talkin, burdies … Ah'll jist keep gettin aw yer pals in here frae the kitchen … Mer n mer … Come away in … .

Mer n mer … Come away in pigins – good burdies. Mer n mer o yese … Mer n mer n mer n mer … … ***Ther-ye-go*** – *that's yese aw, burdies!*

... that's aboot everybdy noo ... Lots n lots o ma wee rainbow burdies fur Mammy ... That's it – make yer wee noises. *Make them louder – everybdy shout loud – 'moan ... Brrrreew, brrreew ... Brrrreew, brrreew ... Brrrreew, brrreew ... Ay – louder!*

Wait – ah hear somethin! Ther's somedy at the door, burdies. D'ye hear them knockin oan the door? Ah'd better go tae ask who's ther. Mammy says no tae open the door tae strangers. *Never, never.* Keep the chain oan until ye know who it is – check it's them first afore ye take the chain aff.

H lo? **H lo?** *Who's ther? Ma Mammy says no tae let emdy in.*
"Wher's ye'r Mammy, Patrick?"
Ma Mammy's in hur bed. Say yer name – who's that?
"**It's Boabby, Patrick.** *Ye know* ... **Boabby Carruthers** *– fae yer Mammy's work* – the security man that guards the cornflakes doon at the BestShops store. Ah wis jist wonderin if ther's anythin ah kin get yese. Has yer Mammy got the flu? She never came in tae hur work this mornin."
She's sleepin. Dae ah know ye?
"It's yer big pal Boabby, Patrick ... D'ye no remember we went tae the fitba thegither?"
Naw – ah don't like fitba. Ah kinny remember. Dae ah know ye? Whit day is it?
"Ye know ma mither-in-law – Ina – ye know Ina, don't ye? She's yer Mammy's pal ... She lives upsters fae yese. Here she is tae talk tae ye."
"Hello, Patrick ... *it's Ina* ... Where's yer Mammy, son..?"
"Ina, **Mrs Ina!** *In-ye-come-Ina.* Ay ah know ye. Ye're ma Mammy's pal. Ye bring *biscuits.* An ye gie me *choclate.* Ma special choclate – *black* choclate wi' *orange* cream in the middle. Whit day is it?
"It's Thursday, son. Noo that ye know who am ur – yer Mammy's pal – ur ye gonnae open the door fur me?"
Thursday? It's Thursday! Mammy's no up yet! ... *that's bad* ... *that's definitely bad!* Definitely bad! Ah cann'y think. Whit am ur tae dae?
"Jist open the door, Patri ... "
The phone! The phone's ringin ... no stoppin ... no stoppin ... Whit am ur tae dae? Whit am ur tae dae?
"*Open the door for me Patrick, son.* Ye know yer Auntie Ina. Ye know who ah am. Take the chain aff. Ah'll use the key yer mammy gave me ... "
"**Naw** – Mammy says no the chain ... *check first* ... "
"But ye *huv* checked, Patrick, son – ye said ye know m ... "
The phone's still ringin! Whit huv ah tae dae Mrs Ina?
Mammy – Mammy! The phone – quick Mammy..!
... Mammy ... waken up, Mammy ...
Mammy! Ye're sleepin' too long ... the phone
Mammy! Mrs Ina's here, Mammy.
Get up, tell her 'Come away in ... '
Mammy – MAMMY!

Rab Wilson

Translations from the Satires of Horace
Buik 1 Satire 1: The Rat Race

Why are men aa sae disjaskit at thair joabs? Mibbes they're jalousin they'd raither be daein sumthin else. Yet if gien the chaunce tae chainge they'd maist like knock it back. They say they juist pit up wi thair work so's they can pit a wee bittie by fir their retirement. But sic men aften work oan e'en when thair pension's aa made up. Bi l. 40 this disjaskit feelin is directly couplet tae the greed o gowd. In the main bit, (l. 41-107) Horace cracks wi a ticht-fistit miser wha pits furrit sindry airguments in defence o greed. Then the openin theme retours in modified form. "As a result o jeelous greed few fowk can say they've hud a happy life."

Hou come, Maecenas, that naebody is happy wi their lot –
nae maitter gif they'd chosen their career fir thaimsels, or it hud
only happent bi chance – sae they're aa jeelous o ither fowk's joabs?
"It's aa richt fir thae entrepreneurs!" says the sodger,
forjeskit wi the years an worn duin wi servin his kintra.
The entrepreneur, wi his ship row-chowin in the teeth o a strang
Sou-westerly, screichs oot "E'en sodgerin maun be better than this!
wan chairge, an in a meenit it's aa owre, daith or glory!"
The lawyer thinks the fairmer's better aff, especially whan some
briganer comes chappin his door in the wee sma oors.   10
The puir auld briganer, taen fae the sticks an hault
afore the beak at the heich coort, sweirs that city fowks hus goat it made.
Tae quote aa the ither examples ah could gie ye wid tax e'en
                              that auld blawbag Fabius.

But let's cut tae the chase! Here's whit ah'm sayin:
supposin God wis tae say "Richt ma mannie! Here ah am.
                    Ah'll grant ye aa yer weeshes.
You that wis greetin aboot bein the sodger wull nou be the entrepreneur;
you that wis murnin aboot bein a lawyer wull nou be the fairmer, OK?
Aa swap roond an aff yeez go. Whit are yeez waitin oan?"
They'd aa knock him back in a meenit,
                    e'en tho they wir gettin thair hairt's desire.
God wid tint his reason aathegethir,   20
tear oot his hair bi the ruits, an richtly sweir
"That's it! Tae Hell wi the bluidy loat o ye's! Stick aa yer prayers up yer arse."

Ach, we shouldnae lauch aboot it – it's no some jokin maitter –
but then, if it's the truth we're spaikin, whit hairm tae hae a bit lauch?
A haunfae o sweeties an some fun wull aye mak the weans
stick in aa the better at thair ABC's, wull it no?

Aa jokin aside but, nou settle doon, let's get serious fir a meenit.
Thon fairmer, wi his tractor an pleuch, delvin the sile,
thon crookit baurman, thon sodger, thae sailors, bravin aa the elements
o the seeven seas, aa o thaim endurin a life o sair darg,
                                        sae that when they're auld   30
they'll hae a bit pension tae retire oan, and can rest easy.
The same wey thon wee ant that they're aye measuirin up tae
trails aathing he can wi his mou tae add tae the bit pile that he's biggin,
heavin awa tae store somethin awa fir the future.
Then, when the years wheel turns drearily roond tae Winter,
the ant nevvir sets his fuit oot o his door,
but leeves unco blithely oan whit he hus gaithert.
But you – Winter's cauld nor Simmer's heat
can divert you frae yer money-grubbin weys; fire, tempest, sword –
nuthin stauns in yer wey, nae chiel is mair bienlike nor yersel.   40
Whit's the pynt in haein sic a haip o gowd an siller that it maks ye
sae timorsome ye've tae gang an howk a hole in some field an bury it aa?
Ye think: "Gif ah touch a penny o this ah'll suin be doon tae ma last bawbee!"
Gif ye dinnae brek in oan it then whit's the pynt hivvin it?
Supposin yer mill hus thresht a hunner-thoosan bushels o corn,
it disnae mean that yer waim'll haud ony mair nor mine.
Gif ye were hanklet up in a chain-gang an happent tae be the yin cairryin
the piece-bag oan yer achin shooders, ye widnae get ony mair tae eat
than the fellah hanklet next tae ye wha cairriet nocht.
Gif ye leeve within Natur's leemits, whit maitter gif ye hae a hunner or a
thoosan acres unner the pleuch?   50
Och ay, ah hear ye – "It's guid tho, tae peel the sponduliks aff o a big fat wad!"
But if we draw the same amount frae oor wee pile,
then whit maks your big granzies better nor oor wee male-kists?
It's like gin ye were needin a gless o watter, an ye said,
"Ah'd suiner draw it fae this big river than frae that piddlin wee sheuch,
e'en though the amoont's juist the same!" Am ah no richt?
That's hou fowk wha like mair nor their fair shares
gets swep awa, bankin an aa, bi the ragin spate o the Aufidus,
the chiel that juist taks whit he needs, disnae end up drawin
watter that's clarty wi glaur, nor dis he get droondit in the flood.   60
Thair's mony fowks enticed bi desires that evvir an oan begowk thaim.
"Nuthin's eneuch," they say. "Ye're only worth whit ye've goat in yer haun."
Whit can ye dae wi a man lik that? Ye micht as weel tell him tae gae oan
bein miserable, since he enjoys bein a miserable scunner.
He's lik thon rich Athenian miser wha luikt doon his neb
                                        at whit puir fowk hud tae say,
"Ay, they aa sneer at me," he'd say, "but ah aye hae the last lauch,
when ah gae hame at nicht tae keek in ma cash boax!"

Tantalus drouthilie strains at the watter lappin roond his mou –
Ye're lauchin! 'Cept fir the name you an him's taurred wi the same brush.
Scrapin yer siller-secks thegithir ye fa asleep oan tap o thaim, 70
wi yer tongue hingin oot. Objects sae sacred ye daurnae evvir open thaim,
gie ye as much pleesuir than gif paintit oan canvas.
Dae ye no ken whit gowd is fir? Whit pleesuirs it can gie?
Ye can ging oot fur breid an veg, hauf a litre o wine,
an aa the ither needcessities that we cannae dae wi'oot.
Or mibbes ye prefer tae lie wauken at nicht, hauf deid wi fricht,
spendin yer days an nichts in dreid o briganers or fire – e'en yer ain workers
wha ye think micht rip ye aff an piss aff wi aa yer loot?
Fir masel? Ah think ah could dae withoot thae blessins!

But then, ye say, whit if ye catcht the cauld, 80
Or some ither malady that lays ye up in yer bed, ye send fir somebody
tae sit wi ye, runnin wi hot-toddys or send fir the doactir,
wha'll then come an get ye back oan yer feet,
                                   return ye tae the bosom o yer faimily.
Dinnae you believe it. Yer wife an son'd baith love tae see ye aff!
Friens an neighbours, young or auld, they aa hate ye.
Money! Ye made that yer God, nae wunner naebody
gies a toss aboot ye. Whit huv ye duin tae deserve love or respeck?
Or tak yer relatives, mind you, ye cannae aye pick thaim richt eneuch,
but if ye ettled tae haud oan tae their affections
it'd be as daft as ettlin tae train a Donkey 90
tae answer tae the bit an expec him tae win the National.

Sae let's pit some leemit tae this greed fir gowd. As yer walth growes
sae yer dree o puirtith diminishes, an wance ye've goat aa that ye need
ye shuld begin tae wind things doon a bit. Else ye'll end up
lik auld Ummidius. Ah ken, ah ken, but hear me oot, it'll no tak lang:
this Ummidius wis sae rich that he didnae coont his money,
he weichtit it! An he wis that steengy his claes an body wir aye bowfin!
An yet tae his deein day he wis conveenced he wid
end up in the puirs-hoose. At the feenish he wis murdert wi an aix,
swung bi a whoor he wis in tow wi, frae Clytemnestra's kenspeckle clan! 100

"Whit dae ye want me tae dae?
Leeve lik they twa wasters Naevius an Nomentanus, an blaw the bluidy loat?

Ah, noo ye're comparin things that are different
aathegethir. When ah'm tellin ye no tae be a miser
ah'm no sayin ye should juist gang straicht oot an pish it up the wa insteid.
Thare's stages atween the timorous moose an the michty lion, ye ken.
Things are aa set oot in proportion. Thare's leemits tae aathing;
Gif'n ye step ayont thaim, aither side, then ye'll still no be richt.

Tae get back tae ma pynt: must evriwan, because o greed,
be at odds wi hissel, an jeelous o aa thae fowk in the ither joabs;
wastin awa because his neebour's goat produces mair milk than his; 110
an insteid o comparin hissel wi the thoosans worse aff,
he struggles tae ootdae first that yin syne the next? Houevvir fast he rins
he'll aye fin yin that's a wee bit richer in front o him;
lik thae chariot teams at the Colosseum when they loup fae the stalls,
each driver pressin lik mad oan the man that's aheid o him,
blinly ignorin those ahint him that faa's back wi the lave.
Sae it is that we haurdly fin a man wha can verily say
he hus leeved a truly happy life, an wha, when his nummer comes up,
blithely lea's the warld lik the dinner guest wha's cantily etten his fair share.

Ah think ah've said eneuch. Ah'd hate ye tae think that ah'd herriet 120
the works o thon auld bluid-shot Crispinus, sae ah'll no say nae mair!

Buik 1 Satire 2: Houghmagandie

The satire explores the notion that in tryin tae avoid ae moral faut fuils juist end up daein the exac' opposite (l. 24). Frae line 28 oan aa the examples are o a sexual kind, an it becomes clear that the main theme is folly as opposed tae guid sense in oor sexual ongauns. This is maist likely the earliest o the satires, an certies the bawdiest. Nane o the English commentators prents mair nor the first 28 lines. Alexander Pope screivit a glegsome imitation caa'd 'Sober Advice from Horace'!

The federated female flute players union, pedlars o quack meidicines,
hailie sorners, lap dancers, comedians an aa that loat, are owrecome

wi grief at the daith o Tigellius, that weel kent coamic singer –
a furthie true-heartit worthy an sadly lamentit frien. This miserable bugger
owre here houanevvir, fir fear o bein caa'd a spendrif, wid refuse
an auld crony the price o a cup o tea or e'en a bit heat at the fire.
Gif an ye ask anither, left a fortune bi his auld man,
why he's blawin it aa oan heich leevin an stowin his guts,
reivin the shelves o Marks & Sparks fir aa kin o growthie scran
wi money he's mooched, he'll tell ye he disnae waant label't as a   10
ticht-fistit grippy miser. Some think he's great! Ithers ca him an arsehole.

Fufidius, wi mair laund an money than he kens whit tae dae wi,
hates bein label't a baw heidit waster, or gettin taen a lend o.
He chairges 50% a week oan the money he's lent, an hounds
aa the puir buggers tae daith that owes him a single penny.
He taks IOU's fae daft young laddies wha dinnae ken better,
thinkin they ken it aa an brekkin their mither's an faither's hairts.
Aa thaim wha thinks they ken him say, "My God!
ye'd nevvir ken tae luik at him whit he's worth". Yet ye winnae believe
hou hard he is oan his-sel.
                            Thon fellah in that play that Terence wrote,   20
the yin wha turfs his boy oot the hoose an's torchirt wi guilt aboot it,
e'en he's less o a masochist than Fufidius.

Noo, gin onybody speirs, "Whit am ah gettin at here?" ah'll tell him.
In haudin wide o yin faut, ye'll likely faa intae anither.
Thon Maltinus minces aboot lik a big shirtlifter,
whiles anither frames his macho intentions in his ticht jeans,
that chancer Rufillus reeks o eftirshave, Gargonius stinks lik an auld goat.
Thare's nae middle wey. Thare's some wullnae touch
a wummin unless she's as pure as the Well o Spa; ithers prefer
thae hard faced whoor's wi faces ye could split sticks wi.   30
Ootside the massage parlour yae nicht, when this big celeb comes oot –
Cato, nou he's some boy, eh? He shouts "Keep up the guid work ma man!"
Then adds, "Gin a young fellah's baws are burstin fir a tuimmin
then he's richt tae frequent that sort o place. At least that
wey he's no shaggin some ither fellah's wife".
                            "Ah hope ye dinnae think ah'm lik that,"
Cupiennius says. (He likes his manto in thair schuil uniforms!)

Listen tae me, you boys wha love seein two-timers caught wi
their pants doon, ye's dinnae ken hou hard it is fir thae boys.
They cannae win, their pleesuir spiled wi the chaunces they tak,
                            e'en gif they   40
dae get awa wi it, oaften as no, it's no worth the risks they tak.
Wan boy ah ken hud tae jump aff a ruif, wan goat kickt tae daith;
yin wha wis rinnin awa goat jumpt bi a bunch o neds,

anither peyed oot a fortune tae shut some grass up,
wan endit up buggert bi some druggy psychos; there wis even yin
wha goat his tackle (baws an prick an aa) chappit aff wi a sword!
"Perfeckly legal!" said the feck o the fowk. Galba didnae agree.

Is it really safer cruisin the singles baurs fir the fuitloose an fancy-free?
Sallust, noo he's crazy aboot thaim,
juist as ithers are fir the mairriet yins. Noo, if Sallust hud the sense   50
he wis born wi, an fine weel he can afford it (an be better thocht o fir it),
he could easily pey fir some lassie's services
an avoid aa the hassle he gets. But he smugly pats hissel oan the back
an craws: "Ye nevvir see me wi a mairriet wummin".
He's juist lik Marseus, Miss Newcome's boyfrien, wha brocht hame
a lap-dancer ae nicht an introduced her tae his faimily – he boldly statit:
"Ah'd nevvir hiv ocht tae dae wi anither man's wife".
Whit a neck, eh? But he'll go wi whoors an strippers
wha'll rob him blin an rype his pooches. Ye'd think he'd hae
mair sense, he jouks ony adultery but fails tae avoid the wan thing   60
that really maitters regairdless o aa – yer ain self respeck!
Gin ye drag yer faimily's guid name through the glaur, dis it maitter
whether yer pairtner's a mairriet wummin or a twenty quid hooker?

Villius wha, thanks tae his girlfrien, Joy, wis Sulla's son-in-law,
goat taen in bi some heich-class crumpet. He suffert fir it
tho – goat an awfy kickin, wis whackt wi a sword, an hud
the door slam't in his face whilst Longarenus wis upstairs wi her.
Imagine him, faced wi aa this, then hearin the voice o his cock
sayin: "Whit are ye daein? It disnae maitter
tae a staunin cock whethir yer bit manto's descendit fae   70
a michty consul, or deckt oot lik a lady?"
An Villius would say: "But dae ye no ken wha her faither is!?"
Big deal! Juist follow Natur's advice an ye'll no gae wrang.
Much mair sensible. She hus riches tae gie,
gin ye hae the sense tae see it, an dinnae taigle up the halesome
wi the hairmfu. It disnae maitter, dis it, whethir
the trouble's yer ain faut, or ayont yer control? Stop
chasin mairriet weemin, else ye'll regret it. Ye may fin
the price ye've tae pey ootweighs ony pleesuirs ye get.
She micht be deckt oot in geegaws lik the Queen o Sheba,   80
but that'll no gie her a straichter a leg than Cerinthus boasts o.
An whiles the twenty quid hooker can bate thaim aa.
She disnae disguise whit she's sellin, ye can aye
see whit's oan oaffir; she'll show aff aa her guid pynts,
but she'll no hide her bad pynts either.
Thon Arab sheikhs hae a guid trick; when buyin a horse they fling

a blanket owre its heid, fir fear they micht get taen in, sae that
their een gets drawn awa fae ony defect,
an begowkit bi its finer pynts, its sma heid an its heich neck.
Ay, they're no sae daft. Ye should ne'er judge the finer   90
features unner a microscope, then be as blin as Hypsaea
tae its glarin fauts. "Whit airms! Whit legs!" Then finnin oot
she's ill-contriven, ill-natur'd an ill-faured.

Mairriet weemin dinnae mak it obvious tae ye tho. They like tae
kid oan thay're respectable like – unless she's a Catia, o coorse.
If ye waant forbidden fruit that's hidden ahint a wa (an that's
hauf the attraction bi the wey) ye'll aye fin thair's snags, be it
her pee-heein workmates, her pals 'juist drappin in' –
troosers an taps ye cannae lowsen – a hunner an wan things
stoppin ye fae gettin yer hauns oan the guids.   100
Noo, wi yer whoor there's nae problem. She's bi ordnar
hauf-naukit fir a stairt, sae nae chance o her hidin somethin –
baundy legs, plug face ... ye can aye check her oot.
Or aiblins ye'd raither get taen in, an be fleeced
o yer money afore ye get a chance tae check the guids oot?

         The poets sing o the hunter
trackin the maukin throu deep snaw; then when he sees it
lyin thair, he disnae touch it. It's the thrill o the chase, he says:
"Same wi love; it rins past whit's ready tae haun, an eftir flees awa".
Dinnae think sic crambo-clink wull dae ye ony guid tho,
get rid o the tapsalteerie dirdum in yer heart.   110
Wid it no be better tae ask whit leemits Natur pits
oan oor desires, whit haurdships she can thole, whit will gie her
pain, sae we can sort oot the fause fae the real?
When ye've a drouth lik an Arab saundshoe, dae ye insist oan
a gowden tassie tae drink frae? Gif ye're stairvin dae ye turn up yer neb
at aa but steak an lobster? When ye've a taffee-haimmer
in yer troosers an a young rent boy or hooker is near-haun,
an can hae either, wull ye juist shoot yer load in yer breeks?

No me! Ah like houghmagandie when'er ah waant it, nane o yer
'No the nou', or 'Ah waant mair money', or 'When ma man's awa'.   120
It's lik Philodemus says, they kind are aa richt fir the Gauls; he likes
the yins that ur no unco dear, an come straicht aff when bidden.
Mind you, she should aye be a trig an sonsie craitur tho, weel turnt oot,
though ye dinnae waant her tae owerdae things either.
When a wummin slips her left side unner ma richt,
be she the Lady Ilia or the Coontess Egeria; ah can caa her whit ah please.
Nae fear when ah'm oan the joab that her man'll appear,
smash the door in, dugs barkin, pandemonium aa roun,

shoutin, screichin; the puir lassie, white wi shock, loupin oot
o her bed, the fancyman yellin his heid aff, aabody in terror,   130
the guilty mistress fir the ruif owre her heid, me fir ma life,
rinnin barefuit an hauf-naukit fae the hoose, else
ma cash or ma arse, or ma guid name hus had it.
Ay, it's tough gettin caught boys; e'en Fabius wid gie me that!

Buik 1 Satire 9: 'Chancer'.

Hou Horace, oot daunderin ae mornin, rins intae some chancer wha claims tae 'ken his faither', an's ettlin fur Horace tae gie him a knock-doon tae Maecenas. The account is aiblins based oan a rael-life incident, but the character hus nae kenspeckle features that mak him staun oot, an attempts tae name him hae pruived howpless.

Ah wis daunderin alang Sacred Way, gaun owre in ma heid
some daft bit o haivers, as ah aften dae, an fairly taen up wi it,
when this chancer, wha ah kent only bi name, comes up
an grups me bi the haun.
        "Hullaw, auld china!" he says, "Hou're ye gettin oan?"
"Juist fine," says ah. "Weel, ah'll mibbes see ye then!"
        But ah could see he wisnae tae
be pit aff, sae ah gets in first: 'Wis there somethin ye wir eftir, frien?'
"Ay," says he, "ye should get tae ken me. Ah'm an intellectual, ectually."
"Guid fir you!" says ah.
        Desperately ah ettled tae get awa frae him.
Ah stairtit walkin, but duis the bold chancer no baur ma wey.
Ah whispert in ma servant's lug, a cauld sweit rinnin doon ma back.   10
Peyin nae heed, the chancer rattles oan; dae ye ken this place?
        Dae ye ken that place?
gaun throu the hale A-Z o Rome! "Nou keep the heid!" ah says tae masel.
"Ah Bolanus, hou ah envy thon het-heidit temper o yours!"
He jaloused ah wis takkin nae notice; "You're gey keen tae be aff!" he says
"Ye neednae try an kid me oan. It's nae uise tho; thair's nae escape!
ah'll stick tae ye lik glue whaur'er ye gang!"
        "Nae need tae tak ye oot yer wey," ah says.
"Ah'm juist gaun tae veesit an auld frien – wha ye dinnae ken –
he's gey ill in bed, awa across the Tiber, nearhaun Caesar's Gairdens."
"Ah've nuthin better tae dae," he says, "an ah'm fit as a flea.
        Ah'll juist tag alang wi ye."

Ma lugs drapt lik a thrawn donkey gien   20
too heavy a load fir his back. Oor frien went oan,
        "Gif ah'm ony judge o maitters
ye'll fin ma freinship's as guid as that o Viscus an Varius.
Thair's naebody ye can name wha can write as much verse as masel,
nor in sae short a time eithers! Ah'm the brawest dancer in toon,
an e'en Hermogenes wid kill tae hae a voice lik mine!"
This wis ma chance: "Hae ye nae hame tae gae tae?
Dis yer mither no ken that ye're oot?"
"Naw, thair's naebody at hame, ah've buriet thaim aa!"
Lucky fir thaim! ah thocht, that only lea's me. Juist feenish me aff tae!
A weird doom cam back intae ma heid, that an auld Sabine spae-wife

hud telt me when ah wis a boy. Shakin her urn this wis whit she chauntit: 30
"Nae deidlie pussion or traicherous blade wull dae him in;
Nae pechin lungs or kirkyaird-hoast nor pally-fittitness;
His wierd wull be – that the causey-clash wull wear him oot;
Lat him jouk aa sic clishmaclavers when he's grown tae manheid!"

When we goat tae Vesta's temple it wis weel ayont nine – the time
he telt me he wis tae mak a coort appearance; gin he didnae
he wid loss his case. "Dae us a favour auld frien," he speirs.
"Could ye no staun as a character witness fir me, eh?"
       "My god! naw!" ah says. "Ah could ne'er manage
tae staun up in coort. Ah huvnae a clue aboot legal ongauns,
and ah'm in a hurry? An ah've aareadies telt ye whit ah'm daein." 40
       "Och, ah cannae mak up ma mind," he says.
"Dae ah gie up ma case? Or dae ah gie up oan you?"
"Oh, mak it me, *please!*" ah insistit. "Nevvir!" he says, "Ah widnae hear sic
a thing! "Ah doot it'll hae tae be ma case that gaes!" an he boldly steps
oot in front o me. Ah ken when ah'm bate, sae ah follow't oan.
       "Hou dae ye get oan wi Maecenas?" he speirt,
"He's a fine judge o character is he no? An aye picks his friens richt cannily.
He's ridden his luck tae the vera tap, fir shair. Nou, if ye wid only gie
me a knock-doon tae the big man, ah'd dae aa athing in ma powre
tae help ye oot. We'd mak some team, eh? Me an yersel?"

"Ye've goat the wrang idea o hou we cairry-oan up thair," ah says.
"Thair's naethin faurer awa frae your kindae malversit ongauns.
It disnae boathir me that sae an sae's mair weel read   50
or better aff as masel. We've aa got wir ain position tae uphaud."
"Awa! Ye're kiddin!" he says, "That's fantastic! Ah can haurdly believe it!"
"Ah'm telling ye, it's the god's honest truith!"
"Weel, that juist maks me aa the keener tae get acquent wi the great man!"
"Nae boathir!" ah says. "Juist mak a weesh! – A man lik yersel wull juist blaw
him awa. He's that easy taen in, he juist maks oo tae be a bit o a cauld fish."
       "Ye'll no fin me the waantin.
Ah'll bribe aa his servants; an e'en if the day they baur the door oan me
ah'll juist bide ma time, hide in his coal bunker, ambush him in the street
an tak him hame! – *Only wi haurd wirk can ye howp tae bear the gree!*"   60
       In the middle o this performance
wha should appear but ma auld frien Aristius Fuscus, wha kent
this chancer fu weel. We stopt. "Hullaw," he says. "Whaur are ye gaun?"
Ah telt him the score rugged at his sleeve, squeezin his airm (it turnt blue!),
noddin ma heid lik a daftie, an winkin at him – "Get me oot o here!"
But the big man wis enjoyin the tear, an left me tae stew.
Ma bluid wis bilin: "Ah'm shair thair wis some urgent private maitter that ye
waantit tae discuss, wis thair no?" ah hintit.

"Ye're richt!" he says, "But it'll haud tae a day when ye're nae sae thrang. Onywey, it's the Sabbath, the day; ye dinnae want tae upset the Jews?" 70
"Och, ah'm no the religious type," ah replies, weakly.
"Oh but ah am!" says the bold Fuscus. "Ah've no your strang convictions! Juist a puir sinner. Ah'm sorry, Horace, ah'll tell ye next time ah see ye."
Ah weesht fir the groun tae open an swallae me up. The big bugger rins awa an lee's me tae twist i the wuin. Suddentlike, the chancer's rival frae his coort-case appears oan the scene. "Whaur the hell dae ye think ye're gaun? Ya crook!" he roars. Then tae me: "Will you act as a witness, buddy?" "*Ah'm yer man!*" ah says. He then huckles the chancer aff intae the coort. Thair wir cheers aa roond, fowk cam rinnin aa airts.

An that, ma friens, is hou Apollo rescued yours truly.

Illustrations by Neal Cranston, also illustrator of Rab Wilson's Omar Khayyam,

Not Just for the Exercise
Donal McLaughlin

The first two months of 2003 were amazingly good to me. First, Scottish PEN selected me as its first-ever Écrivain sans frontières. *Weeks later, I was selected for the Robert Louis Stevenson Memorial Award. It's an honour to follow in the footsteps of Dilys Rose, Chris Dolan and Gordon Legge.*

The above, from a National Library press release, captures the spirit in which I spent October and November 2003 in Grez-sur-Loing, at Hotel Chevillon, where RLS spent three summers in the 1870s. Unusually for writers from Scotland, I was allocated not Apartment 4, but the Carl Larsson House – in the garden behind the hotel. "Famous Swedish painter", a Swedish translator explained to me – 1853-1919.

From the moment I first stepped into the garden to approach the house, I knew how difficult it would be to leave. The setting was stunning. Shades of green I associated with May in Scotland welcomed me as, down through the trees at the foot, I saw the River Loing, golden in late afternoon sunlight, hardly move, it seemed, beneath the arches, the stone, of the famous, much-painted bridge. In among and just beyond the trees were the knee-high stumps of their predecessors: seats for a group to sit and listen in the sunset; the glade; a magical auditorium.

The house had a terrace looking onto the lower half of the garden. French windows in the living-room opened onto the same. Upstairs, the bedroom's double balcony again looked onto this view. To the right was the Tower of Ganne; from this angle a chess-piece; a grey-sandstone bishop. Ahead was the river; on either side of the bridge were the plains beyond the trees lining the Loing; then more trees. I stretched and breathed, unable to take it all in. Below was the 'inn-garden' which in Louis' day "descended in terraces to the river; stable-yard, kailyard, orchard, and a space of lawn, fringed with rushes and embellished with a green arbour". This was also the setting of the famous photograph of Fanny Osbourne, reclined across an upturned boat or two down by the jetty, surrounded by seven or eight men, behatted, jacketed, with cousin Bob in his striped socks, easily identifiable, and Louis, for some reason, missing.

There were no ghosts, though. The Stevensons, the Glasgow Boys, the Larssons would make their way in later. I was raring to do what I'd come to do – to see what I could make of recent experiences in Latvia. It's mad, I kept thinking. *Short stories* have brought me here; have earned me this. From cluttered desk in my front room to this!

I begin to read. Alasdair Gray, *The Ends of our Tethers*. The man's in great form; each story a treat. 20kg was my baggage allowance, so Aleksandar Hemon's *The Question of Bruno* and *Nowhere Man* are my only other books – Latvian books, for research purposes, apart.

I set up my PowerBook in the huge artist's studio upstairs. There's a work surface at the window to the street; another, larger still, brighter, beneath the window to the garden. I opt for this; sit down at the Powerbook as if in a huge barn. Ulf, Swedish video-maker, and Paul, Finnish painter, are soon teasing me about having this work-space. "The biggest and most expensive – and you don't even paint!" I hear, daily.

On Day 5, a birthday breakfast for Ulf brings everyone together. Ulf, his photographer wife, Johanna, and baby son, Otto, are descended upon. Otto, not yet one, steals the show: his plucky attempts at walking; later, to play the piano. The Swedes speak English for my sake. Soon I'm flicking through Gerd's folder: her book in progress. Have received a catalogue of her husband Hasse's work. Paul, Ulf and I will regularly coincide in the TV corner – with the telly off or ignored. Cracking conversations are had. We young turks agree the Finn is tops: Paul, an avid reader with a wicked sense of humour and hilarious stories galore; who has acted in films, was in Paris in '68 and has worked in Florence, Rome, Paris, New York. Though 20 years our senior, he works out and cycles the canal route to Nemours. Paul, who knows his stuff; whose test we want to pass; who, more than anyone else, brings the different folk here together.

The others remark how quickly I've settled to work. Painters take time to set up their studios, then have to work out what they're going to paint. Ulf has equipment to shift back and forward daily between his studio and car. "It's easier for writers!" these artists guess. "You guys just take up your laptop and walk. Set it down somewhere and carry on writing." I've just done an edit of *Lanzarote* – and there's a danger that the style and voice might colour the new project. Soon I'm re-reading *Treasure Island*, *Kidnapped*, wowed by the man's ability to tell a yarn. Finding *Franklin's Grace*, an Irish short story anthology, soon has me thinking about that form too. The trick will be to break free from what I wrote before.

The library, mainly in Scandinavian languages on Scandanavian subjects, contains works donated by writers who have spent time at Chevillon. The walls are adorned with artworks produced at the Foundation. Everyone leaves something behind, I was told on Day 1 – a point reinforced each time I cross the chessboard floor of the the main hall.

In October the first-ever *Journées Stevenson à Barbizon* are held. Saturday 18 October sees the inauguration of *La Promenade RLS* – a walk in the footsteps of Bob and Louis between Grez and Barbizon (the tale is told in 'Forest Notes': of how their walk "for the exercise" became an ordeal). Bernadette Plissart (who runs Hotel Chevillon) leads our group on a 2.5 hour walk from Grez, Christilla Pelle-Döuel (organiser of the *Journées*) leads a larger group on a 3-hour hike from Barbizon. Readings are held and bagpipes played at the Carrefour des Grands Feuillards. Etienne Fernagut of French-Swiss radio reads passages by RLS in French. I read the beginning of *Treasure Island* in English. A section of my own story 'aka La Giaconda' is read in English and French.

The next day a panel of five, Swedish novelist Björn Larsson, and writers Jacques Meunier, Anne Vallaeys, Alain Dugrand and Christilla Pelle-Döuel, discusses the importance of Barbizon, Grez and the forest of Fontainebleau for RLS. Michel Le Bris has had to call off. Björn, the author of *Long John Silver* (Harvill), emphasises Stevenson's ability to tell a tale. This Swedish writer acknowledges how he's tried to *study* Stevenson's technique, only to be sucked in and swept away by the narrative every time. Jacques Meunier offers some abstractions, challenges my knowledge of French. Alain Dugrand responds, with frequent reference to Conrad. Anne Vallaeys answers questions about the forest, then and now. Christilla cannot be beaten when it comes to biography. It's the women who keep this debate anchored.

Etienne and I close the event with a bilingual reading of poetry, Jacques having handed me *Pas moi!* (*Moral Emblems*) the evening before. It warms the heart to read for Jacques – this *gentilhomme*, this *ethnologue et écrivain*, friend and peer of Chatwin and Bouvier who's contributed to *Le Monde* for 20 years. I'm glad to read for a man who puts me so at ease; who leaned on his stick as he asked about my work, my first impressions of Grez and shared so easily his knowledge of things I didn't, couldn't, know. I lost count of the number of people who whispered to me that Jacques was *très malade*. He told me himself. And that he was undergoing *chimio*. Only months later, his friends are now recalling how Jacques took himself into that forest that day, despite being *malade*. They take comfort from the fact that his last public appearance focused on RLS; that he lived to see the inauguration of the Promenade. *Lorsque meurt un homme comme ça*, his obituary in *Le Monde* concludes, *c'est le groupe entier qui est lésé, amoindri*. In 2004, the *Journées* will be dedicated to his memory.

The *Journées Stevenson* impact greatly on me: I'm reading RLS from the outset; make excellent contacts and wonderful new friends who offer much in the weeks that follow. Just days later I'm told I've been 'adopted'.

End of Month 1, when Swedish friends leave, I see the *Livre d'Or*. The pressure's on: to design an entry which captures your time in Grez. *Mais seulement si tu veux*, Bernadette stresses. Flicking through the guest books, you realise how much has been created by so many people in Grez. I'm just glad that new things are happening. I see the difference when I revise stuff written before. The forest air works wonders.

In Apt 1, Ingrid (Ingemark) is busy translating: from English, Mary Laven's *Virgins of Venice* or Norwegian, Lars Saabye Christensen's *Maskeblomstfamilien*. Paul (Osipow) is painting his ruins – or cakes from the local *boulangerie*. Early evening, if I'm lucky, I'm chosen to eat his *models*. Hasse (Ekdahl) paints his headless suited men in colourful landscapes, while his wife Gerd works on the book which will combine her tapestries and paintings with text. Batte (Sahlin) arrives to produce water-colour versions of Hill's famous steps. His wife, Birgitta (Gahrton) is a fellow translator. I show them the BOSLIT database; listen to their comments as we view what exists in Swedish. The last Swedish feature on contemporary Scottish writing was done in '96 – something we plan to change.

Ulf (Lundin) is out filming in nearby villages and towns. *Je ne parle pas français*, it's called. If someone agrees to be filmed, he switches on the camera. It's then for them to end the process. Ulf stands back and waits. We discuss the implications; the different reactions of people. This is the man whose camera pried (by agreement) on his best friend's family for a year (*Pictures of a Family*, 1996). Who filmed people sneezing (*Bless You*, 1999). Who watched them sneeze to know when best to film. I sense similar moments in writing – bits of *Lanzarote*; of "surviving uncertain fates".

I visit Paris once. At the Louvre, umpteen black-and-white photocopies of the Mona Lisa lead me and a circus of others to *La Giaconda*. The pilgrimage, for me, is necessary (see *Edinburgh Review* No 111). Paris, I can do on penny flights from Prestwick, I decide. I'm happy to stay in one place. It's no hardship when it's so idyllic. I'm reminded of Earl Lovelace, from Trinidad, at the Book Festival in '98 – reluctant to leave the site; happy to view Edinburgh from the spot, the yurt, he'd found.

The walled garden becomes my realm. "There is 'something to do' at Gretz", Louis wrote. If there is, we've missed it. There's *nothing* (which is fine; which is *the attraction*). Ulf teases me about missing the hot-air balloon, the only excitement in his first month. Conversations can focus on the most trivial of details: coping in French; getting from A to B; or where to buy or eat what. Visits to the *boulangerie* become an event. News bulletins are filed regarding the owner, now known as *Madame Baguette*. Her son provides the town's only spectacle: the disco lights in his bedroom. I joke about my world being reduced to my desk, the garden, the river, the ducks. "*Il y a de l'eau*, as people have said", Louis wrote. Ingrid, whose apartment looks onto the street, reports on how nothing happens either on the *Place de la République*. The so-called square houses the Bar Hotel La Terrasse (due to re-open on 9 November) immediately on the left; the Café de la Poste (Presse/Tabac) further along; the bakery on the right; and Post Office at the far end. It's a *street*. And as for the alleged population of Grez of over a thousand, we've seen twenty-odd, max. You know it's Wednesday, Ingrid notes, when Mme Baguette's lights don't come on, first thing. On Wednesdays, there's no *pain au chocolat* or *un comme ça* for breakfast. On Wednesdays, Grez is closed-closed.

This slant on the world takes hold and I'm thinking about making use of it when Chris Dolan's email arrives. Is that amazing video still in the library? he asks. The one made in Grez on 9-11? I fish it out and we hold a spontaneous viewing. *Meantime in Grez*. Ylva Floreman, the director, arrived on 9-10. From her apartment, probably, she filmed the street outside, only rarely moving the camera. The film consists of 'stills', on which Ylva superimposes text messages sent to and from Sweden.

Meantime in Grez: 12 minutes which offer a breath-taking slant on 9-11 and force you to reconsider how you live and work (a) normally, and (b) in Grez. The opening shot shows La Terrasse by night, obviously open when Ylva was here. "Here at last. Great room. Quaint place. Perfect!" a first sms declares. Images follow which we know: the bakery first thing in the morning, two dogs tied up outside, leaping to greet their owner when he re-emerges with bread; Mme Baguette's son on his balcony, donning his jacket. Images we don't know follow: Baguette junior performing conjuring tricks in the room with the flashing lights; a 'sailor' settling down at white tables and chairs outside La Terrasse; Baguette Jr's face in close-up, bathed in red light. Then the first sign something's wrong: old men in the street pointing, their talk clearly agitated. A message is received: "plane crashes WTC. turn TV on – Mom". The white cat on the window sill; the red shutters of La Terrasse. "don't believe it".

The drama increases. Eva texts from Sweden: "check out TV. NY hit by terrorists". The bent man we recognise drops his crutch to lift litter from the pavement. "Scary for passengers. for those at WTC. for us. for world." With his one crutch, he hirples to the litter bin, manages to deposit the litter. "This is just the beginning".

We see La Terrasse by night again, next. The streetlights are on. Mme Baguette's son is juggling – balls – in his lit room. "I want to go home. to Sweden," Ylva texts – and cats scream beneath Baguette Jr's balcony. The camera registers the boy's alarmed look. A women chases the cats below. Church bells ring out nine o'clock above the deserted square.

Morning dawns again and the bakery prepares to open, its light the only sign of life. "Don't speak French. TV dubbed. What's up?" The man with the basket ties his dogs to the wall again and enters the bakery. "Bush wants to retaliate", Sweden informs Ylva. A man climbs out of the blue car. Two teenagers on rollerblades sail down the middle of the road. "Will this be World War III?" the next sms asks. The 'sailor' pats the ginger cat, its tail now erect. "War – Please come home – sis". Mme Baguette's son looks out over his balcony. A pedestrian waves to a car to slow. "What if I get stuck down here?" Ylva asks. A man with 2 baguettes crosses the road. The bent man on crutches struggles off to the right.

"Relax Drink Wine Enjoy France Mum" we read as a circus arrives in town. We see lionesses in cages. The tannoy announces a spectacle "mercredi à 15h" – *pour tout le monde*. Four men sit smoking outside La Terrasse. Are still there in the evening beneath the street-lights when guitarists begin to play. Mme Baguette's son's disco lights flash in his room; others jazz up the shutters outside. "Fear mustn't prevail. No more TV" an sms announces. A man in a T-shirt, smoking, has spotted Ylva's camera; plays to it. At La Terrasse, only the white cat is still outside. A singer's heard from within; then laughter. "I'll stay put," Ylva decides.

Another morning. Heavy rain falls on Mme Baguette's son's balcony.

The dogs and an erect black umbrella await their owner outside the bakery. The brolly moves in the wind. The dog-owner gets under his umbrella and then frees the dogs. The poodle in the red coat's on its hind legs as, possibly, we hear thunder. A white car works its way down the street. Pedestrians carry brollies which remain down. "Back home. Grey skies and 50 degrees. What's up?" The white chairs are now stacked outside La Terrasse; aren't needed in the rain. We see the cat outside the restaurant, by night again. "Life!" comes the reply as Baguette Jr juggles – skittles – bathed in blue light. There's a dog outside La Terrasse as the shutters next door are closed. The guitarist we hear one last time as the final credits roll.

I rise from the sofa – to rewind and remove the video. The odd sensation I feel is shared, exchanged looks would suggest, as – silent, for once – we return to whatever we do.

Month 2: a new bunch of Swedes arrive whom Paul and I, in Bernadette's absence, welcome. Katarina von Bredow, a children's writer, Åsa Moberg, novelist, journalist, translator of Catherine Millet into Swedish. Åsa's architect partner Bror. And Barbro Öhrling, a painter.

Barbro and I work late; our evening shifts coinciding. We often chat in the library but I don't know what she's painting. I've seen her long white coat by the river and postponed walks not to disturb her. One evening, her door's open. I see paintings on the wall. She's painting *what I see*. Has focused on the same group of trees; their reflection in the water. Suddenly, it feels right to tell her. To discuss what she does. Then Gavin Bowd arrives, fellow Scot, working on Michael Scot, who also knows his Houellebecq. Who teaches, speaks French, whereas Paul and I merely try.

I learn more about the Larssons, about Hill and his tortured drawings (produced on paper bags), dip into books on RLS by Bell, Calder, Knight and Stott. Paul introduces me to Richard Holmes. Soon, I'm reading French. Michel Le Bris on RLS. Alexandra Lapierre on Fanny. Initially, I wanted to be able to answer Swedish questions. Now I'm wondering whether I might set something in Grez. Philippe Delerm's short novel *Sundborn ou les jours de lumière* allows me to imagine Larsson and Co here.

Autumn has arrived. We saw the signs as the first Swedes prepared to leave. Walking in the forest, alone, the eyes in the back of my head peeled for wild boar (or: *sangliers*), I've seen those May greens turn to autumn; leaves take their place on the forest floor; leaves shower down up ahead to form rare splashes of gold; shades of grey now dominate where once were delicate greens: barcodes where once was pointillism. Mistletoe asserts itself in the skeletons of trees; smoke issues from the piles of leaves burning slowly along the canal. Finally, the trees are bare-bare. I see further ahead, around, and sense how foolish I was. The dreaded sangliers could've been anywhere as I savoured what felt like Spring.

Swans fly along the canal, in pairs. The electrifying whoosh of their wingspan is new to me. I see a heron land in a tree. Observe the etiquette of anglers, joggers, dog-walkers. The kid in me kicks his way through a field of chestnut leaves each time I reach Nemours. Light fades rapidly as I return to Grez and so I avoid the forest. The canal keeps me right. The final stretch on the main road I do in darkness, knowing not even headlights scare off *sangliers*. How to react if you encounter one is something I've asked about. Thankfully, the only one I see's a dictionary illustration.

11-30, inevitably, comes. In the days before, Xmas decorations go up in Nemours; are even turned on. Madame Baguette's son has Santa climbing in through his bedroom shutters, too. I've done Halloween and autumn here. It's time to move on. My last ten minutes are spent down by the river; the Hotel, the full length of the garden, behind me. Barbro and her boyfriend are lingering up above, are observing this farewell. My over-heavy suitcase stands upright, outside what was my door.

I study the water, the ducks. The trees that Barbro paints.

I inhale the last of the air.

I've no doubt whatsoever: Grez has been very special. I reflect on the people I've met. Their work, their support and encouragement. The things we have in common. The things we all commit to.

It's time to take that home. To ensure I, too, protect it.

Donal McLaughlin – photograph by Marc Gaber (Riga)

at the poolside
Donal McLaughlin
Two extracts from Lanzarote: a novel in progress

In Part 1 of the novel, set in December 1998, Kevin Rainey and Craig Scott travel to Lanzarote for Christmas. Operation Desert Fox begins only hours before they depart from Glasgow. Kevin narrates.

Next mornin, the sky's back to its bright blue sunny best. Normal service is resumed: when I head off to fetch breakfast, I return to find the table set. Craig comes out lookin ready for five sets of tennis.

The better weather brings the neighbours out. A guy the spittin image of your man in *My Name is Joe* turns up. He doesn't say owt to us two but when his pals turn up, the end of the war's the talk of the poolside.

"Blair and Clinton's just called it off!" Joe announces. "Eleven o'clock on Saturday night! They're claimin victory. Or at least: they're sayin they've done enough to make their point; to teach Saddam a lesson."

He doesn't get much of a response.

"Ye can't do that, if ye ask me. Ye can't go to war wi sumdy 'n' then claim victory even though ye've no defeated them."

There's still no response. It's like folk are acceptin, more or less, what he's sayin. At most, they nod.

"Taught Saddam a lesson, my arse! Ye canni dae that. It's like they set oot tae gie him six o the best 'n' ended up lettin him off wi two –"

People look up, this time; surprised by the image.

"Ah kin jist see Saddam chucklin away tae hissel. Goin back to his wee pals, showin them his hauns, 'n' givin it: it wisni even sair – !"

His pals around the pool laugh.

"They've said, Blair & Clinton, they'll resume the war if Saddam gives them cause –" Mr Perthshire intervenes. "They've stated quite clearly that military action will be resumed if he again defies his international obligations."

"Ay – and meanwhile they'll be savin up their pennies, the money back on lemonade bottles, for Round 2, like?" Joe says. "Cos that's what all this is really about: the readies; the finance!"

"Can't argue with you there!" Mr P concedes.

The Ger looks out of his depth; doesn't contribute. I keep *stumm* the fact I was out demonstratin, in '91. Even went to Glasgow for the big demo. It's no just Saddam my quarrel's wi. There'd be no need for this war now, and that war then, if America and Britain hadn't built him up in the first place. If we're goney talk justified reactions, let's look at our own reactions much earlier down the line, that's what I say. That way, you don't have to go to war lookin like fuckin hypocrites.

Joe, it turns out, is the type of guy who can't keep himself to himself.

Has to share whatever he finds funny wi whoever's around. He gets a response out of Craig. If it were up to me, I'd ignore him. Craig takes him on but. Every time.

An hour or so into the session, I have to laugh: Joe's just watched Mrs P do Mr's back. Quick as a flash, the chancer's round to that side o the pool wi his suntan lotion, askin if she'll do him, too. Mrs P laughs, takin the bottle. Doesn't even look at Mr. She gets on wi it, quite the thing, while the Rangers fan shouts across, slaggin Joe off. Mr P looks vaguely embarrassed; can see the funny side but. He gets his say by agreein wi the Ger.

Joe sits there, lappin it up; his love handles hingin over the top o his shorts. He looks at us two, wi a big grin, like he's tryin to tell us what we're missin. Once Mrs P's finished, Joe dives straight into the pool.

"Ay, ye probably need to cool down, ya fly bastard!"

The Ger's still givin him a hard time.

Mrs P turns to Mr. They chuckle at what's happened. No harm done, they seem to agree. No harm in it.

That said, Mr P looks like his patience is stretched when Joe climbs out & is straight back over wi the bottle again.

"Ye shoulda thought o that afore ye jumped in!" the Ger gives it. "That nice woman might do it for ye. Don't think ye're comin runnin to ma Carol but!"

Mrs P gets on wi it – though it's pretty clear it's a top-up job and no the full works this time.

Joe, meanwhile, beams at the whole poolside.

"Ay, lads! A woman's hands! Nothin like a woman's hands!" he grins. "Why do it yirsel when a woman can do it for you?"

The rep turns up.

Between one thing and another, she hasn't seen us yet.

"Alright, boys? Enjoying your holiday?"

"Ay."

"Yeah, great, thanks!"

"Well, I'm Caroline. Anything I can do to help! Any questions you might have, I'm here to help. My times are up at Reception –"

"Cheers, thanks."

We look at each other as if to say *Won't be needin her.*

We take pride in no turnin up for Welcome Events. Do our own thing, that's us. Nay cunt's holdin our hands. We'll suss the island ourselves.

Early afternoon, the last poolside regular turns up: a greyin blond from Dublin. A would-be sophisticate, it's written all over him. Gay, probably. Joe seems to know him. From here, that is. Not know-know.

"Good night last night, Richard?"

"Did the trick, my man. Ay, it did the trick!"

"Late back were you?"

"Late enough, Ay – "

"Didn't see you comin in, so I didn't – '
Joe's fishin, but he's had as much as he's gettin.
Craig pops inside. Comes back out, unasked, with lunch.
"Ya beaut!"
Partisan rolls & chunks of cheese & chorizo he'll have used his penknife to cut. I tuck in. Grab the chance to top up the suntan lotion when I take in the plates. One advantage o the poolside over the beach: way you can just nip in to the mirror or fridge.

We carry on sunnin. Craig's readin a history of Scotland; something he's always meant to do. Only two books he has wi him are histories. Spot the non-fiction man! He told me on a previous holiday he devoured *Ladybirds* as a kid. Would read for general knowledge, but no otherwise. Didn't – doesn't – want to know about fiction. Too subjective, he says.

Doesn't stop me: I'll be gobblin down novels like they were stories.

Only excitement's at twenty to four. I know it's that time cos I've just looked at the wee alarm clock I keep by me to time the suntan lotion.

At 3:40, a tall slim black guy walks into the complex. He causes a stir, specially since he's entered from the rear. He's no come past Reception. It's like he's sneaked up on us from behind.

He's maybe more our age than Joe's, but it's Joe he speaks to. Maybe cos Joe's at the poolside, feet danglin in the water, & is first to clock him.

When they don't understand each other, the black guy hands over summit someone's written down for him.

"Oh – it's Richard you're lookin for!" Joe says, suddenly soundin like the top man in a old-style tailor's. "Richard's in No.11 –"

The guy still looks totally lost; confused.

"Richard – Number 11 – along there –" Joe repeats, pointin.

Before the guy can move but, Richard enters the scene, carryin a poly bag. He's been to the supermarket. *Reina Sofia*.

The whole pool's watchin. No explanations are needed.

"Four o'clock, I said!" is all Richard gets out. "I said four o'clock – you're early!" He takes the boy along to the far end of the pool – no that there's any distance involved. It's more like a plunge, sure. This way, he's no right next to Joe & Mr & Mrs P, at least.

"Are you no goney introduce us all to your new friend, Richard?" Joe asks, pointedly.

He doesn't get a response.

"Stick then – be like that!"

A number o us make halfhearted attempts at our own conversations to ease the tension. They're no half as manufactured as Richard's, though. We're all tuned in, o course, wi one ear, to that.

After what Richard must reckon's a respectable period, he offers the boy tea. The boy accepts, and they make their way in, wi the air o two gentlemen about to have a cuppa.

"Tea, eh?" Joe says wi a big dirty wink to the rest o us. "That's me bombed out o my place for the next hour or so. Who knows what I might hear through the wall?"

"Ay, yir right there, mate. It's naw fake fuckin watches that boy's sellin, that's for sure!"

Craig turns to me. "You have to feel for him!"

"Whit?"

"Poor guy just popped out to buy something nice for a cup of tea – and the young guy turns up early and embarrasses him – !"

Game, set, and match to Scott again. He's forever sussin situations like this.

"Is there no situation you can't read?"

He laughs. "Just a nosey bastard, mate. That's all!"

The sun goes down, wi no further sign of Richard.

"Longest bloody cup of tea I've ever heard tell o, I'll tell ye that!" Joe says as he rolls up his towel to go in.

That night, on the way to the restaurant, we look out for the Sunday papers. Or I do.

SADDAM BUSTERS CALL OFF THE WAR is the version we find.

What we read doesn't tell us much more than what we heard at the poolside. The discourse these cunts can come up wi when they want to!

There were no British or American planes lost in the four-day action, they're sayin.

The Grave

In Part 2, Kevin Rainey, an Irish Scot, returns to Lanzarote alone. He becomes increasingly interested in the life and work of the painter, sculptor, architect & environmentalist César Manrique (1919-1992).

This was what he got for takin it into his head to visit Manrique's grave: drivin round in circles he now was, tryin to find the thing.

A plot o land with a low perimeter wall containin nothin but gravestones shouldn't be hard to spot, he'd thought. None o his books revealed the exact location; he'd been confident he could guess, but. Travellin north, comin down off that spectacular helter-skelter carved into the hillside, it would be on the left o the road that led into the town. Comin south from Mirador del Rio, it would be to the right as you emerged from the narrow streets round the town hall. He was still able to visualise what that bit looked like. Was convinced the cemetery would be in there, somewhere.

As he hit Haria from the south, he veered left. Initially, he found nothin but a maze o tiny streets. Some roads that looked like they might lead somewhere proved to be dead-ends. Others led into private property. They were all so narrow. He'd visions of endin up in a ditch; of locals haulin him out. The heat o the afternoon was startin to do his head in, 'n' all. The number o times he thought he was in first, only to discover he was still in third, and that was why it wouldn't shift!

At one point, he thought he'd found the place; that he'd spotted it, off to his left. Relieved, he headed towards it, only for the road just to stop but. Unable to drive where he wanted to; afraid to park where he wanted to; he dumped the car & walked. He might as well not've bothered. The nearer he got, the less he could tell about the place. The entrance, when he reached it, was sign-less; the huge wooden gate was locked.

There was nowt else for it: time for other options, it was – maybe off the road north. There was a route *to* Mirador del Rio through Haria; and another, slightly different, *back*. He knew both from before and was gettin to know them better; the overlap, especially. What was needed, something was tellin him, was an option *off* this road. No matter how often he drove back and forward but, he hit on nothing that helped. The municipal crematorium, aye. The hill down into Maguez, aye. If it was them you wanted, you were fine. The cemetery, but, must've got up and walked. Nothing he attempted would take him there.

The crematorium was like a bloody magnet. There was no gettin away from it. Landing back for the umpteenth time, he relented; decided to ask someone. In luck, he was. Any other day it might've been deserted; today but, the men seemed slow to leave. At the main entrance, four or five hogged the shade, anyway, while others stood out in the sun. Not one looked a day under seventy. Fewer still would know any *inglese*. He'd have to ask them, but. Language barrier or not, he *had* to.

He got some odd looks as he opened the gate. More still, as he wandered right up. "Any of you speak English?" he asked, gently.

He didn't get a response. The sun belted down as he showed them he could wait.

"¿Themeterio?" he asked. He'd seen the word on a road sign; the question was how to pronounce it.

"¿Cemeterio?" he ventured, when still no response came.

A toothless mouth began to move within a haggard face. He watched it, transfixed. What he was hearin could've been "This is the crematorium, mate, not the bloody cemetery!"; or "Think we tell tourists where our cemetery is?" He was damned if he could understand a word but. The speaker fell silent again.

Wherever Kevin looked, eyes – from beneath hats – now pierced him.

"¿Cemeterio?" he asked, one last time, in desperation.

This time the guy began to wave – in the direction of a local hillside.

"Over there, is it?" he asked, hopefully.

"Sí. Sí."

"And how do I get there?"

He got there. The ghost of Manrique must've interceded again; there was no other explanation. All he knew was: next thing, miraculously, he's on a different road. And on the bend, behind high walls and a church-like entrance, is – *Bingo!*

He pulled in to park & saw a solemn-looking guy with a pony-tail leadin his partner out. Early thirties, maybe, they were; no strangers to dance floors & parties. Their recent bereavement had aged them but. The grief, you could see, was hers, mainly – your man was hoping to ease it. The hurt, you could see, was still raw. Even from a distance, this touched him. Something inside him dissolved – he could *feel* it – as he watched what were strangers depart.

CALLE VISTA DEL VALLE, the sign above him read. "View of the Valley", that could mean. If so, it wasn't kiddin. Most of the palmtrees, the famous thousand, had to be visible from here. His gaze panned the slopes. Lingered on the houses; all white. On the greenery; the palms; the hillside. Manrique had lived here, spent his final years here.

The church-like entrance he'd seen from the car consisted of an archway, with a cross & inscription above it. YO SOY LA RESURRECCION Y LA VIDA. He entered to see black crosses, white crosses, wooden crosses: crosses, wherever he looked. Over to his left, he spotted the kind of set-up he knew from Gran Canaria: the graves Craig had compared to luggage-lockers in stations. Here, too, were walls of plaques, with the dead, presumably, behind them. Row upon row of them; four high. Each slot, the regulation size & shape, no doubt. The plaques black; cold; marble, mainly. And barely a flower to decorate them.

At his feet was a different style: the horizontal slabs of maybe older graves, stretching to the rear of the graveyard. Some bore inscriptions. Others had boxes, numbered, on which the different coloured crosses were erected. Beyond these, in both back corners, were chapel-like structures: altars with the slickest of crosses. The white walls contrasted with the black ash, he noted. Trees added splashes of green.

He inched his way forward, resolved to be systematic; to search for as long as it took. The small stones crunched beneath his feet. Almost immediately, he spotted the palmtree & remembered the newspaper stuff Craig had discovered. Of course! The grave was beneath a palmtree! They'd seen it in that old *Lancelot*! He'd forgotten that collage, in the meantime. In among the headlines but, the front pages from that September, had been images from the funeral, also. The one of the grave came back to him now. Odd, it had been. Too much of a snapshot. Making the grave look too small; too fresh; too *makeshift*.

He needed to focus, he told himself. Was about to stand at the grave. Was in no doubt at all, now, he'd found it. The palmtree had grown some, in seven years; so, too, had the cactus, at the foot. Approaching, he recognised the shape more: the long low casket-shaped plot. C.MANRIQUE, he read, finally – the letters carved in volcanic stone; a brown stone from the island.

"Thanks, César, man," he thought. He maybe even said it.

He'd the cemetery to himself. There was nothing, nobody, to get in his way. He stood there, thinking – gratefully, he realised – about all the man had done. The fact he'd done it at all; the fact he'd done it *from here*. He got thinking, too, about what the guy had *stood for*. Drifted from that to what mattered to himself. Standing there, quietly, he felt – as rarely before – the courage and a resolve to live by that; to work by that.

He was touched to see others felt similarly. *Du lebst in unserm Herzen*, the ribbon on a wreath declared. Someone had left colourful beads; someone else, a bracelet. Three roses had been put on the grave, as had been shells, stones, pieces of rock; even arrangements of tiny pebbles. A handwritten note lay beneath a stone. Its spidery blue writing caught his eye. It was okay to look, he decided. As he stooped – *belleza* – to lift it, he was able – *sensibilidad* – to decipher some words. A page from an oldfashioned writing pad, it was, he realised, unfolding it.

His Spanish was non-existent. He could glean, though, that, for the author, standin at the grave was a moment of sadness and emotion. With all the love he could muster (it was a *he*, it had to be; an *elderly* he) – with *all the love he could muster,* he wanted to say *thank you* for all the work, all the beauty, Manrique had created; for the things he'd done for the island. Manrique, it went on, had shown islanders how to be proud of their island; how to show Lanzarote to others. The next bit was about defendin it from foreign aggressions, or something. Then came references to *serenity* and *delicacy*. To *sensitivity*. To Manrique's *perfection of communication* and *medium*. The final words were *Hasta siempre*. Below that was just something illegible.

"Yeah, thanks, César," Kevin thought – again.

He replaced the note, but didn't leave immediately. Instead, he caught himself stalling; as if to find a way back to his own thoughts and feelings.

When the time came to go, he picked his way out, past the many many crosses. Manrique was buried in a *churchyard*, it now occurred to him. The fact was suddenly an issue. His was the only grave without a cross but. Was the only grave with a palmtree.

He reached the exit and looked back. From here, the palm looked part of a *group* of trees. What was once a tiny plant had grown; matured. Was now part of its environment.

He walked back to his car. A mother and daughter were preparin, at theirs, to visit the grave of a loved one. He'd had peace and quiet to do what he'd wanted. Now they would have the same.

Some way down the road he was before he thought to put a tape on.

> *that palm and cactus:*
> *in the funeral photo,*
> *no size; now, some size*

George Hardie

The Kiwi Wha Becam the Auk
For Sydney Goodsir Smith, (1915-75)

Ye, whause antipodean vyce
suld be a sair rebuke ti us
wha suld been born ti prize
the leid ye uised sae bonnilie.

But, mind on this,
ye were iver free o aa the edication
we had ti endure for ti ensure
a fully blawn (the better ti get on)
richt guid gaun de-Scottified North Briton.

I ken, I ken – we hae been uisan
that excuse sae mony year
it's worn ti near transparencie
     the daunce o seiven veils
     wi ae veil left
     and whit's ahint's a sicht
     wad gar ye boak
     and hae ye switchan aff the licht.

And sae, I raise my bunnet and my gless
ti aa yer wild lampoonerie,
yer blauds o braw buffoonerie
yer haliket absurderie
yer blousterous braw-wurderie
that tuik oor antient leid
and, wi a shairp and skeely glead,
gied it a heist whan it was needit
and schawed the wey it suld be heidit.

But ye left us faur ower suin

The faut was niver yours but oors
wha roupt the rowth o bonnie flooers
an cuist thaim on the midden flair
wi nocht but little thocht or care
sae tentlesslie.

If, at the hinnerend o aa
I chaunce, bi luck, ti meet wi you
and aa thon rumptious makar crew,
up by Kynd Kittoch's howff,
I'll faa ti mak defence.

A want o genius I'll conceed
(nae man wad argifie)
an ootlin frae thon blessit breed
(thon waal's, lang since, rin dry)
an yet aethin thay maun alloo
altho, aft times, the starns were few
Guid save us, Sirs, I tried

Stormy Wather

The bloustrous win lays the whip o the rain
doon ower the ruif's rigbane.
The windaes flinch and flude wi tears
doors grit thair teeth and willna gie.
While I, wi pen in haun,
gawp thru the greitan gless
at the surge and ebb o the clashan trees
across the lamp-post's watery licht
and wunder whaur I'll fin a poem
on sic a rammasche nicht.

The Clydeside

The river, on a sun-bricht spring,
skinklan aneath the caller air
past raw on raw o trees
braw in a bleeze o blossom
wad turn, cum autumn,
ti the rowthe o fruit for Glesca
and thon ither Clyde.
Syne, ti sclim the brae, turn
and see the sun skime and skimmer
on a sea o gless whaur, in the growthie damp,
plants wad rise ti shouther the wecht
o gleamin reid tomataes
   – the best thare iver was.

I'm mindit o the laddie,
wad jouk inbye at grampa's
   him lettan on
   he didna ken that I was thare
luikan for the anes
had burst thair sides wi lauchan
and, o a sudden, realise, thon laddie,
or pairt that niver quite grew up
is still aboot juist waitan ti be foun.

Fairm Dugs

Thonder thay cum, the beasts,
reekan in the dreich and drizzlie wat
drappan a mix o dung and glaur
makan a midden o the dreipin road.

And the men ahint, reekan an aa,
thair draibbelt duds
near as slaigert as the beasts,
thwackan thair sticks
and shoutan, aye, in a tung
anerlie the beasts mun unnerstaun.
Guid kens I niver had the maisterie.

But, gin ye meet thaim
thay'll greet ye wi a nod and,
    "Haun oot the road, man
    or thay'll hae ye ower."

But see and mind the draigelt dug.
Oh, sleekit brutes, the fairm dugs.
Wad let ye bye syne,
wi a snapperan snarl,
hae yer ankles frae ahint.

Staun ti the side and let thaim bye, and
    "Rab, cum oot o that,"
'll save ye o a chawan … mibbies.

The Makar's Weird

The makar's weird it is ti scrieve
doon bi the laich sea's edge
syne hae his words obliterate
bi the neist tide's tentless surge.

Thare are a few, a seilfu few,
'll hae thair words engraved
aye bidan on the grenit shore
as thay were yet brent new.

But, for the lave wha ettle yet
ti ply the gangrel trade
sum fleetin glisks o simmer sun
is aa we're like ti win

and wi that minimum o praise
contentit we maun bide.

Ugly Duckling

Carol McKay

They met up again outside the Planetarium. He was standing by the pillar. If she watched from beside the gravity well she could see him before he saw her. He stood with his back to her, expecting her to come along the length of the sloping glass front that ran with water down to the river every time it rained. *Nice weather for ducks*, he would tell her.

A girl with blond pigtails and fluffy pink baubles rolled a penny into the gravity well. Anna watched it circle till it eventually *plunk*ed into the darkness. The girl pleaded with her father for another coin.

Anna glanced towards the Planetarium. He was still waiting, his shoulders too big to be concealed behind the pillar. She could see his toffee coloured t-shirt – the smart one – and the light beige jeans he wore because he liked the anchor buttons. His fleece was in the crook of his arm. She went to him when the queue started to move.

"Hi," he said, leaning slightly to brush her cheek with a kiss that smelled bitter as orange rind. "Feeling better?"

"Fine." She tried a smile. His hand was heavy on her shoulder.

"Ready?" His eyebrows almost met in the middle and his face was thick skinned and waxen.

"Ready." Anna didn't mind while the Planetarium wasn't completely dark. He sat in the middle beside the projector and she sat beside him with their jackets on her other side. The seats leaned back to allow an easy view of the stars. The first time she'd likened it to the dentist but he'd stretched his legs out as if he was sunbathing. She watched him now as he crossed his ankles, right foot over left; elbows on the chair arms – taking the one between them without even asking. His hands were clasped over his waist and he was still wearing his ring. Anna cast her eyes over the audience, gauging their mounting excitement. For her the stars had lost their sparkle. Well, these ones. The sky was green above them, a sickly green thrown up on the perfect dome by bulbs concealed in a recess in the walls and the stars when they came out were just a con.

"Sit back and relax," he told her. She shook her head and sat, prim almost, hands clasped in her lap, checking for the member of staff.

"Enjoy yourself."

It sounded like an entreaty. She willed herself to say something, knowing it was time this stopped. "I want –"

Too late. The presenter walked to the front of the hall and Anna lay back, trying to be as blank as the sky overhead. Nettle sting tingled under her arms. The presenter dimmed the sky from twilight to dusk and the spectators chattered like birds then hushed. The presenter said if anyone needed help she would shine her special torch. They should just call out.

Anna wanted to shout, but in the middle of the row, in the black of the auditorium she knew she had sunk too deep. Her hands gripped the arm rests, the inside of her wrist brushing his warm forearm. Her eyes flared to let in any flicker of light but there wasn't a glint. Just his slow breathing. And then his hand, clamping over hers. His hot palm. There were spots of light on her peripheral vision. The red dot from a torch journeyed across the ceiling heading for Venus, the evening and morning star on the Western horizon.

The presenter started her monologue. Anna was word perfect. She knew how long it took. Venus is the brightest star. Sacred to lovers, it marks the boundaries of the time for lovers to love.

She felt the tug of each anchor button. She let him pull her hand on to his lap. She felt his clamminess in the curl of her fingers; the pasty coolness of the spheres.

Venus has a poisonous atmosphere. He slid his thick finger under the elastic of her waistband. She quashed a disloyal bud of excitement and dug her nails in to make him stop. Repulsed, she worked him harder, efficient, practised, devoid of other options.

Venus is a planet not a sun and it doesn't twinkle. She felt him writhe. She covered his face with his fleece and he mouthed at her fingers through it. The red beam journeyed through the Milky Way's thin white scatter. Anna wiped her hand, lay back and travelled in the constellations: Venus was in Virgo. Her favourite was the Cygnet, flying east to west along the course of the river. But it was just an illusion.

Outside, he asked if she wanted coffee but she needed to wash her hands.

Two girls were looking in the mirror. They were about her own age and wore their hair in bunches. It made them look young. Anna washed her hands in the too-hot water till it stung. She wiped away steam and looked for a resemblance but there was none. Between him and her, between her and them. She was ugly and she didn't fit in. She took off the sweatshirt he'd bought her on his last trip, held it between her knees while she brushed her hair off her face and into bunches but even that didn't make any difference. She let the cold water run. Scooping it up, she damped her neck, letting the droplets dribble down her back. There was only a hot air dryer, so she dried her hands on the sweatshirt instead and stuffed it in the bin while the two girls stared.

He didn't know her when she came out so she slipped upstairs to the top when he wasn't looking. There were trees here and she sat under them gazing out to the river. Someone was playing the songs of birds. She recognised a cuckoo; she didn't hear any ducks. The river moved from east to west past the Millennium Bridge, the helicopter pad and the old sailing ship. Kids played around her under the Science Centre trees.

"Here you are." He sat beside her. It was too late for coffee and she'd been round the gift shop a million times.

"On the ocean," he said, "you can see the stars really clearly."

He told her that sailors used to steer by the North Star, as if she hadn't heard the presenter say that every time they'd come.

He looked out of the window in silence and she saw how his big knee bent out towards her and how his thumbs rubbed over one another in their loose hand clasp between his legs. He sat back in the seat again and studied her. "You look different like that," he said, touching her bunches.

She winced.

"Younger."

When she didn't reply he asked her what she was looking at and she said it was the swans. He stretched his feet out.

"I have to go to sea again," he said, reaching for something in his pocket. "This is the last time I can see you."

She met his eyes as he handed over their season ticket. His eyes were shaded under the heavy black of his brow and she wondered what he would do without her. A leaf that was prematurely yellow dropped between them on the seat but neither remarked on it and he took twenty pounds from his wallet and gave it to her.

"Don't mention this to your mother or she'll be looking for it all the time."

It was almost five o'clock. He put away his wallet and grasped her in a hug that was crushingly awkward. She wouldn't meet his lips or even his eyes but she watched when he left, still carrying his fleece in the crook of his arm. His shoulders were still broad. For a moment she remembered the hot breadth of his neck between her thighs and the uncontainable joy-ride of being shoulder carried, his hands massive around her ankles and her fingers unconsciously toying with his hair.

There were two swans on the river. As she went downstairs she watched them through the clear glass frontage on every level. Outside, she crossed the courtyard to the Millennium Bridge hoping they would still be there. They were. Swans mate for life.

She heard the sound of a child protesting. A girl with blond pigtails and fluffy pink baubles struggled against being lifted to see over the parapet into the flood of dark water, but her father insisted. Her legs flailed uselessly till she eventually gave in.

Anna pulled at the elastics that held her hair in bunches and thrust them in her pocket beside the season ticket and the money he had given her. Her mother would be waiting in the car park with a thin white circle where there used to be a ring.

Anna looked at the big wooden beams that held up the quayside. She looked at the perpendicular ladders leading into the water. She looked at the swans and their cygnets swimming east to west, down the river towards the helicopter pad, the tall ship and the open sea.

Dennis O'Donnell

That Vettriano Touch

The billiard room booms with echoes.
Isolated lamps hang the tables
like emerald visions in the dark.
The beings that flit through the light
sometimes pause, disturbed by the sound
of heavy footfalls on wooden boards.
But, through light into darkness, there is only
the lower half of a coated man,
or the swishing doors after he's gone.

The woman, by herself at a table in the café,
rolling her lips at their reflection
in her silver compact mirror, freezes,
her scarlet lipstick unapplied.
Someone is there at the window behind her.
She sees his reflection in the mirror opposite,
looking in, through Venetian blinds,
from light to dark. The slats of the blind
slice his face – no eyes, no mouth.
The coffee-machine gasps and screeches.

The Sphinx

He feels like he's lived a thousand years.
Not an old man but never young,
and now walled up with memories:

a wooden birdcage hangs in a window
in an old street,
the shutters flaking blistered paint;

a bygone boudoir scented with roses;
a dress discarded; naked arms;

a white building in a fashionable district
that formerly echoed to horse's hooves;
elegant women with parasols
strolling under avenues of limes.

Then the horseless carriage came,
the city grew black and it boomed with noise.

In a room dark with brocaded drapes
he sits with his writing.

And, outside,
the grids of streets roar with traffic;
lights flash and flicker in the night;
the city has grown to the size of a star
in the country's flaring constellation;
images and messages pulse in the aether;
airliners squat against the air,
landing travellers from around the world –
a very small world that turns,
very slowly, among millions of others.

Blue Hotel

Reception is untended at this dead hour.
In the kitchen, the Insectocutor's blue light glares.

The dining-room chandeliers are darkened
but the grand piano's fin surfaces
as a car's lights sweep the farther wall
through the tall windows of black glass.

Carpeted stairs muffle footfalls.
Long, stifling corridors are lit
by lights are harsh as prison lights.
Asylum lights.
            The swish of a skirt.

Guests lie unsleeping in darkened rooms.
A tread blocks the light at the foot of a door.
A fly cracks in the Insectocutor.

Like a Jacobean villain, the night porter
passes the distant end of a corridor.
A target in sights, were there any to see him.

McQuarry lights two cigarettes, passes one
to a sullen stranger in a black slip,
in a hotel room stale with smoke and scent.

Lonely Street

Crossing the enigma of the empty square,
McQuarry turns his collar up
and tugs his hat-brim over his eyes.

A bell tones once, thin and distorted,
and the clockface floats its lurid fiction
high over sunset junctions.

Long shadows. Arches and columns.
The rear view of a colossal statue.

Now the city is blocks of darkness,
distant squares and oblongs of black
with chance mosaics of glowing light.
Traffic lights change at random
down faraway abandoned streets.

An intersection. Circles of light.
A pool hall. A barbershop. A store.
McQuarry stands in a pitch-dark doorway,
watching the place across the street –
a diner, a world glaringly lit
and sealed off from the city outside
by its protective bubble of curved plate glass.

Where two streets meet.
                        Deserted.
A solitary man sits there, hunched,
with his back to McQuarry, drinking coffee.
Later, a couple in their early thirties;
together, intent. Lovers, maybe.
A busboy wipes the counter slowly.
The ghosts have gone. The rain comes on.

Sweep

The chimney sweep came to Ramsay Crescent
when I lived in the house at the top of the brae.
He arrived, outlandish as a nigger minstrel:
white eyes liquid in his blackened face;
lips and tongue lewdly red;
on his shoulder a sooty sack of rods
like the fasces of a Roman lictor.

He knelt by the grate to unwrap his bundle,
then slotted his rods together
and moved the brush up the chimney in sections.
He turned his golliwog face towards me
and his slack, red, smiling mouth
told me my place was on the back green,
to shout out the minute the brush emerged.

After a child's lifetime of waiting,
craning and squinting against the blue,
the brush-head appeared out of the lum,
a sudden demon in a puff of black.

The next time he came, the magic was different.
He climbed a ladder to the roof and dropped
a lead cannonball down the chimney,
dragging his brush down the flues.
On the back green again, I watched Ole Black Joe.
I worshipped him up there, godlike
on the dew-rinsed slates of the morning
while tiers of crescents, streets and avenues
sparkled and fell away from his feet.

Batwing

> *Life is a beautiful and strange winged creature*
> *that appears at a window, flies swiftly through*
> *the banquet-hall and is gone.* – The Venerable Bede

There are no belfries in the village,
no caves where a parliament of bats
might roost, hooked upside-down
like corpses of rats in leather shrouds,

so I had to look several times
at the bobbing black shape
in the gloom of the lane outside the house
before I could be sure it was a bat:

Strauss's Fledermaus.
In Italian it's old 'Pipistrello',
like a flying glove from the Commedia dell'Arte;
to the French a 'bald mouse' in fancy dress
of mask and domino.

A tossed scrap of black brolly,
bent spokes and taut fabric,
it flapped its cloistered, jagged flight
around the old chimneys and outhouses,
a black shape cut in a scissors class,
a shadow figure silhouetted in dusk,
then it flitted out over the garden
and away across the river.

I don't understand why they're held in dread.
Not so much pterodactyls or bats out of hell,
helmeted and goggled, they are
magnificent mice in their flying machines.

Touch Wood

Something about wood is reassuring;
not simply the fact that trees, too, live –
slower and longer,
with roots locked to the underworld.
Even stacked in a timber-yard:
in planks, batons, boards or beams,
its touch, and its smell snag the senses.
Wood is textured, grained and fragrant.

Once, in a faraway summer vacation,
restoring a Georgian Edinburgh house,
I laboured to joiners, that select guild.
They wore their nailbags like masons' aprons;
hammers were thrust daggerwise
through belts. Their mouths bristled with nails.
I watched one planing a window-frame
with long, even, smooth strokes,
his plane of gleaming hickory, pommeled.
Soft shavings curled from the wood
in scrolls and spirals around his trestle.

He showed me a spar from the old window,
split it over his knee, and the room
was sharp with the tang of long-dead glades.
"Yellow Pine," he said on a sigh.
"They don't use it now. More's the pity."

I sat as a boy in the fork of a tree,
squirreled away in the rustling leafage;
safe as a bird in the clinch of the branches
upheld by the massive, greenwood tree,
its bark like the grey and corrugated hide
of elephant or rhinoceros.

The World Tree, rooted in earth,
it moved against the drifting sky
slowly, in tree time, and I was part.
Human time zipped by, unheard,
till hunger spurred me, boyish, home
and I dropped to the world from branches of cloud.

Pelicans
Lee Kofman

When she came out of the shower into the bedroom, she saw her husband's belt. It curved on the bed, a dark brown snake, casting shadows on the white sheets she had always been strict about, the way she had been with fresh flowers in vases and cool home-made lemonade in the fridge.

She heard her husband moving dishes in the kitchen. She had never liked him being there, preferring to keep her meals as a kind of mystery, so he would believe that when she clicked her fingers, capsicums stuffed with red rice, fragrant mince and green dill would land on the glass dining table, designed by her husband's famous acquaintance.

Later on she heard him turning on the stereo. Sounds of electronic music filled the place. He used to say that this music was much more than just music, it felt to him like a sudden infusion of energy. Often he would put it on and then ask her for a dance. She liked it so much, this ability of his to turn everyday things into their little private party. Soon, as was usual in the early evening hours in their spacious, neat apartment, warmth would spread between them. She would put her head in his lap and the external world would seem less scary; and the next morning – when they each turned to their own business – would seem as remote as the galaxies he liked to read about.

He called for her, but she stood frozen in the bedroom. The towel was dropping off her like like a dried bark. They had already been married two years, but that was the first time since she had known him that she could relate the ownership of this item to him. Now she remembered there were other belts of his hanging in the dressing room. She had never noticed them before. She shuddered, terrified, trying to calculate how many of them he actually had. Her husband was the first man in her life, who had shoulders she could rest her head on. Other men she had known (and she had known many before she met him), resembled scarecrows, no matter what their real complexion was. They slept with her and usually also paid for her in restaurants and drove her everywhere she wanted. However in return they all wanted to break down in front of her in the recesses of the bedroom, pass her their tears and failures. They had always relied on her to be a stable beast of burden for their sorrow.

Whereas her husband – before he became her husband and before he even slept with her – had taken off his shirt in his bedroom. His chest was narrow and his skin was white-reddish and overall he was not an attractive man. She started to plan the smoothest way to sleep away from his bedroom, but then he pointed out his gentle shoulders. He said, "If you marry me, you'll always have them. You can lean on me any time."

She understood at once: here was her opportunity to overstep the circularity of her repetitious life.

However now she wasn't sure she knew whom she had married. The coarse object – the one which could whistle in the air – placed a question mark over her new life. She felt utterly exposed in her nakedness in front of his leather belt. All of a sudden she had become aware of the quiver of her white flesh, of its frivolous abundance in some places on her body. If one day the snake lifted its head in her husband's hands, how would she be able to protect herself?

Disgusted, she observed her body, which had always been considered by men attractive, even though it didn't fit the current fashion standards. When she lifted her head, her gaze intersected with her husband's. He stood in the bedroom doorway and watched her nakedness, smiling.

She ignored his smile and said, "You left your belt on the bed," trying to make it sound casual. Then she immediately became frightened. After all, what if even as a jest, as a seductive gesture, he would lash her on his way to the dressing room? How would she be able to look at him again? Would she have to get divorced? She was trembling now.

When they just got married she was in love mostly with his shoulders. When they made love, she covered them with long kisses involving the tongue, sucking and marking them with love-bites. Later his whole skinny whitish-reddish body became attractive to her. It happened gradually, and then one day she understood that without noticing she had become addicted to him, as well as to his excitement in little souvenir shops that offered fruity soaps; or at the street Jazz shows, when he would start dancing in front of the crowd, dragging her with him. She was in love with the way he would always hurry to light her cigarette, just when she touched it; and with his palms which encompassed her face, containing it. His love of life was contagious and she was drawn to him, loading the burden of her past onto his shoulders, much like Scheherezade, and for a similar reason – to save her life. But she had never told him the story of that day, when once again she and her girlfriends – the wild girls in her class – wagged school. As usual, they climbed down the steep path, which led to the deserted beach with no lifeguards. The sea bottom was rocky and had always wounded their feet.

Pelicans would often frequent that beach and the girls would say how those birds with their long throats resembled their classmate's grandfather, who had got that mysterious illness "throat cancer." And she, who had always been considered the smart one, would say, "I'm sure these birds gave it to her grandfather. They carry cancers in their throats. They find them in these deserted beaches, swallow them and then pass them on to people. For them it's like a competition, to see who can pass on more."

The other girls would shudder, checking under their bare feet, whether there were any cancers wandering about, whereas she would put on a serious face, thinking of how clever she was, how easy it was to invent stories and how her stories had that magical power to abruptly change others' moods. It was so clear she had the ability to become a magician. When the silly adults asked her what she would like to be when she grows up, she would shrug her shoulders and say, "A magician, of course." And Mother would get angry and say, "She will be a lawyer."

She loved herself in those hours with her girlfriends on the beach. They used to talk about all kinds of significant things, inhaling the pungent smell of the rotten seaweed and saying it was like the drugs one of their mothers would smoke on the weekends – and that they are stoned now. To demonstrate their stoned condition they would step into the water, swaying on the hard stones and trying to scare the pelicans, which were not really impressed with their little show. The seawater lapped at their feet, easing the midday heat. The sun would smile at them and the seagulls would fly especially low, white like the Christmas angels.

One day their hiding place was discovered and Mother came and talked to the school principal and all the way home held her arm very strongly, hastening her steps more and more.

"So," Mother said to her lover – one of those, who occasionally lived with them – "What shall I do with her?"

Mother had always hoped her lovers would have the answers. Perhaps that was the reason why she had been changing them so often, searching for the ultimate answer.

Her lover, a skinny short man, who never talked much, said, "This girl needs a man's hand." Slowly he took off his belt.

She would always remember her life as being brutally bisected on that day. The whistling lashes had indicated with torn skin and blood the final separation between the "Almighty Magician" and the girl, whose dress could be rolled up just like that and whose panties could be pulled down to expose her pale buttocks. It was then that she ceased believing in her ability to influence the world with her words.

The worst memory from that day wasn't the pain, and nor even Mother's face as she held her hands down and occasionally whispered through her contracted lips, "Want more? Or have you had enough and want to apologize?" No, the worst memory was the powerful way the lover's hands moved when he beat her up. He was a short man with a weak mouth and used to stand on his tiptoes when kissing her Mother. She would never guess he could …

She also remembered how she hadn't been brave the way a wild girl should be. How she had capitulated pretty quickly, screaming under the lashings, her bum prancing quickly, trying to escape the stinging leather snake, "I'm sorry! Forgive me!" But he wouldn't stop, till Mother dropped her hands abruptly, got up and yelled at him to stop right now.

The next day Mother threw him out of the house, but for her it didn't matter anymore. The belt of Mother's lover had annihilated her magical powers for good.

She had never told her husband all that.

He smiled at her, looking her body over. She was naturally shy and never walked naked around the house. When they made love in the daylight, she'd ask him to shut the blinds. At nights she would get up to turn off the lights.

"Sorry," he chuckled, moving towards the bed. "I didn't think it would disturb you ... OK, I'll hang the belt up. By the way, has anyone ever told you how sexy you look after a shower?"

The hand of her husband – the man with the shoulders – touched the metallic buckle. Instinctively she stepped back towards the bathroom. She was shivering again, strained: would he be tempted? Can ownership of a thick leather belt change a person?

Her husband picked up the belt, passing by her on his way to the dressing room. She moved to let him through, but he moved towards her, still wearing his business suit, and pressed himself to her naked body. He said, "Hmm ... You're still wet."

She felt wet down there as well, much wetter than she'd ever been. She withdrew quickly, looking for the towel to cover herself.

And then ... That light and so expected-unexpected stinging on her bottom, when she bent to pick up the towel ... All the blood rushed to flood her face; automatically she covered the hurt buttock with her hand. She wasn't able to move or turn towards him or protest.

Her husband let a choked laugh slip, his well-known prelude to their lovemaking. Behind her back she heard the noise of the belt hitting the floor. Its presence made her mind vague, blurring the borders between her body and the yellowish bathroom walls. She turned towards her husband, who took her in his arms and led her into their bedroom filled with scented candles.

She knew she probably shouldn't be following him now; that their future together would lose its brightness if at that exact moment they sank into the bed; and that her life would be bisected again by a leather whistle through the air. But the flesh between her legs had swelled up more and more and she needed her husband in a way she'd never known before. Flames of candles winked at her maliciously, smelling of rotten seaweed, dragging her down towards the bottom of salty waters. Underneath her shut eyelids a pelican was flapping. She forced herself to open her eyes for a moment and looked into her husband's, wondering who was this man inside her.

The Fairytale of the Immigrant-Writer and the Three-Headed Hydra

Lee Kofman

And the wise man said to the confused immigrant-writer: "Only when you tame the three-headed hydra (and be careful you don't violate any animal rights), will you then be free of the 'writers block' spell."

The first head – language "Yeah …" sighed Simon (in Russian). "And what does it mean?" He quoted in English: "The eastern lamb winked at us from a distance." "Nu, lamb," I responded in a frivolous mixture of English and Russian, coloured by my heavy Israeli accent. "Like the one I have in my room …" "Uh, sorry. I meant lamp. Eastern lamp." "So what do you mean by winked?" Simon sounded tired. "That's not a mistake," I defended myself. "This is my style. The lamb … sorry, the winking lamp is an image." If I were the reader, I'd drop this article now. Luckily I'm the author and, perhaps less luckily, this is my life story.

Simon is a Russian poet who emigrated to Australia 20 years ago. I was a developing writer in Israel, but God knows what I am in Australia. "What's that?" whispered Simon in despair, pointing at the following words: *nekudat hashaka.* "I couldn't find it in the dictionary," I explained. "So I wrote it down in Hebrew." After a heated discussion we discovered it meant 'point of contact' in geometry. Simon and I met after I'd been in Australia 18 months, gradually accepting that I needed to find a new occupation. However, as Dovlatov, a Russian writer who emigrated to New York, said: "You don't become a writer because of the good life you'll lead. This profession chooses its own people." So Simon, who believed in Dovlatov and in doing things your own way, offered to help me learn to write in English. Those were strange days. I'd write a story first in Hebrew, translate it into bad English and then, sitting in the Acland Street cafés, discuss it in Russian to improve the English. I bought dictionaries, thesauruses, idiom books and other aid material. I learned how English words can be tricky, sneaking into Russian whilst being absent from Hebrew dictionaries or vice versa. A word, *ephebi*, that I suspected to be English but couldn't find in any dictionary, appeared to be of Greek origin, meaning youths who have reached puberty, and was in my book of phrase and fable. I also learned that when English speakers say 'bigwig' they don't mean a drag queen or Marie-Antoinette. My English is improving, but reading is tedious, like watching movies in slow motion. It can take me two or three days of reading for the protagonist to finish a meal, depending on the richness of the author's vocabulary.

This is my second change of languages. My first poetic enlightenment occurred at age 3 in Siberia where I was born, when I read in front of the village babushkas: "The blue bird flies up to the sky. The blue bird goes high." They appreciated it. After emigrating to Israel aged 12, I spent my first years there as I do today, devouring books in Hebrew, a dictionary always in hand, not skipping a single unfamiliar word. It was easier then; perhaps because modern Hebrew doesn't have as many words as Russian or English. For the last two years, having begun to get published in English in Australia, I've been working with a professional tutor, a literary editor. I treat our relationship in the same romantic way painters and musicians treat their teachers. This is how I refine my craft.

Writer-immigrants never stop writing in their new countries. Psychology claims that an immigrant's degree of mastery of the new country's language is a direct indicator of their sense of belonging. Usually writers who consider themselves 'in exile' (which means they view their new condition as unwanted or temporary), keep writing in their own language. Writers who see themselves as immigrants, that is, whose move was their choice, will flirt with the new language. They won't necessarily deny their first language, but might become bilingual (or multilingual) writers. Some of the greatest literature by Russian writers of the 20th century was written outside Russia by those who fled abroad after the October revolution or were later expelled by the Soviet authorities. Most of them continued to write in Russian. Those who became known in the West prior to emigration, such as Dovlatov or Solzhenitsyn, could keep writing in Russian, relying on the publishers to translate them. Others waited until the Iron Curtain was lifted to publish in Russia again. Nowadays many Russian writers reside in Paris, New York or Tel Aviv, but sell books in Russia. Even though he had an ambivalent relationship with Germany and enjoyed his comfortable life in America, Remarque wrote his 11 novels in German. We shouldn't forget though that he was famous in America prior to emigration; Hollywood had made movies of his novels, so he could afford the luxury of writing in his own language.

Many writers who have changed the language they write in have had the advantage of prior knowledge. Nabokov had a governess who taught him English from early childhood. The Indian-American writer Bharati Mukherjee received a classical British education while living in Calcutta. On the other hand, Joseph Conrad, the son of a Polish nobleman, knew no English at all when at age 21 he went to sea on a British merchant ship. At 27 he received his British residency and became one of the best descriptive writers ever, writing in English, his third language. Joseph Brodsky, a Russian poet expelled from the Soviet Union in 1972 who emigrated to America, is said to be one of the best essayists in the English language. "To read his essays is to experience English at its finest," wrote one prominent American critic. Brodsky taught himself English in his 20s while still in Russia by reading and translating English poetry. He had a massive English-Russian dictionary and would browse through it again and again, checking every word and nuance. Yet, after arriving in America aged 32, he began learning English again from scratch. Eventually he became a bilingual writer. He saw English as an instrument through which to discover the world; it was as indispensable for him as Russian and that he'd go mad if forced to choose only one language ...

One of the greatest challenges for a writer in adopting a new language is developing a feel for it. Not only was Nabokov a gifted writer, he was also a passionate linguist, fluent in Russian and English, who could write in French and understood several other European languages. This enabled him to play with the meanings of words in varied tongues, and mock both the fussiness of Europeans as well as the bewildered response they evoked in America. Extensive reading of good quality books in a new language helps. Good writers have a sensual and aesthetic relationship with words. They follow their natural music. Using several languages provides a kind of 'brain massage': it sharpens our thinking and our sensory perceptions. I enjoyed discovering that the beautifully elastic word emerald sounds similarly in both Hebrew (*izmargad*) and Russian (*izumrud*), despite the fact that these three languages are all from different origins: Latin, Semitic and Cyrillic. As a fresh beginner you have the opportunity to revive words long forgotten by locals and can avoid the usage of clichés through simply not knowing them.

The second head – identity. The adaptation process for a writer in a new country reminds me of the psychologist Maslow's theory of the Hierarchy of Needs which states that certain lower needs need to be satisfied before the higher needs can be. As soon as you satisfy one, the next one pops up. Several writers I knew in Israel had told me that it was impossible to change languages. When I started to get a feel for the language there wasn't much of a sense of joy and victory – rather the opposite. I had lost my 'technical excuse' (even though I can still whine about poor vocabulary and so on). This was when I was forced to face the scariest head of the hydra, the fundamental existential question all 'tortured artists' face, but which torments you even more when you are an immigrant: What do I have to say and to whom?

The first step in overcoming this panic was to challenge my perception of Australians as aliens. I may be putting my entire future in this country at risk when I say so, but I was so terrified of being too different to be understood that I ignored the fact that we are all made from the same DNA. Perhaps my panic started when I first attended a local writers' group and was told that you couldn't publish a short story unless you wrote something about some small country-town with an old man, a tree and clouds. In Israel my only experience of the country was a park in Tel Aviv. Whereas my main impressions of the country here, in Australia, were the snooker pubs with their old jukeboxes. When I decided out of despair to write this down in an article which was then actually published, I experienced my most significant 'cultural shock'. It was only later on when my short story about suicide bombings in Israel was judged a finalist in a short story competition in Australia that I began to seriously question the writers' group's advice, and especially doubt my own cultural theories.

"My language is my country," wrote Portuguese poet Fernando Pessoa. What did he mean? People often mistake the idea of country for a particular culture, a comfort and sense of belonging within their own *milieu*. Immigrants who find these in their adopted countries still refer to their previous country as their true home. Yet when revisiting it they often describe feelings of estrangement. They feel they are 'insiders, but outsiders' at the same time. Asked whether he would go back to Russia after the fall of communism, Brodsky replied, "You cannot return to a country that no longer exists." Brodsky captured the fluid, non-geographical quality of this mythical country. It is the same elusive country Pessoa was referring to. If culture and sense of belonging make a country, then my country is my imagination. Imagination can be practised everywhere. Readers will always respond to a good story. Many of us grew up on Andersen's fairytales without being Danish.

Immigration can benefit writers in many ways: it is a source of inspiration and can enrich a writer's cultural and philosophical perceptions while presenting him or her with new moral dilemmas and standards. One of the first to understand this was, of course, a Greek. They were always ahead of us. Plutarch, who lived circa 100 AD, once said while trying to cheer up a friend doomed to exile: "Indeed the muses, it appears, called exile to their aid in perfecting for the ancients the finest and most esteemed of their writings". Even though immigration is a stressful experience, it can facilitate the development of a unique voice (if he or she has the initial talent and the originality of thought). Your perception of your new country will be different to that of the locals and your descriptions will be fresh. Conrad brought to England a sense of life's strangeness that was lacking in the Victorian tradition. I particularly enjoy writing about the Casino, as in Israel this is outlawed. Its cheap glamour becomes my personal fairytale. Baraheni, one of Iran's prominent writers, now living in Toronto, claims that writing poetry in another language is an entirely different enterprise which produces different poetry. I think it isn't just language which influences the writer-immigrant's work; it is the flavours of the new lifestyle and pop culture, the different values and especially the fabulous details, such as the ominous (to my foreigner's eyes …) grin of Melbourne's Luna Park.

Baraheni also says that when well-known writers emigrate, they sink into anonymity. He calls this "a tragic loss of identity". But anonymity can also be fertile soil for inspiration. The hardships experienced can be successfully transformed into fabulous fiction – this is how so-called immigration literature originated. A fresh start in Australia freed me from the topics I used to write about (mainly urban violence and loneliness, and post-army traumas) and allowed me to develop new themes and writing style. From a rough and direct tone I'm drifting now towards more soft and dreamy sentences. Perhaps this is also because of this new language's music and how I perceive it. However, this optimistic, even romanticised, view of the migration experience does not always apply. As Goran Simic, a Yugoslav poet who moved to Canada after the siege of Sarajevo in 1996 says: "There is a question of how much a writer can be transplanted from one country to another and survive. It's like a flower. Sometimes flowers can't survive in another country." After emigrating Simic spent two years slinging boxes, tried briefly to run a restaurant business and then retired to live on his savings and write poetry. Marina Tsvetayeva's lines: "On this partially severed rope/ I – a small dancer/ I – a shadow of somebody's shadow. I – a lunatic" make me shiver every time – the lines seem to be a vision of her end. Tsvetayeva emigrated to Paris shortly after the revolution, in 1925, living in poverty, her work mainly published in émigré publications. She alienated herself from the other Russian émigrés when she refused to sign their document belittling Mayakovsky's achievements. Eventually her husband, who meanwhile had found employment with the NKVD (later KGB), returned to Russia. Tsvetayeva joined him in 1938 and the following year her husband was executed. In 1941 Tsvetayeva hanged herself.

The third head – the reductive nature of the new identity. The next danger facing a writer-immigrant who has succeeded in taming the first two heads, is that of falling in love with his or her newly shaped exotic identity. Lavish descriptions of colourful foreign foods, landscapes and traditions cannot stand on their own. Celebration or mourning of the past and the current immigration experience are good themes, but they should not be cultivated high on pedestals cut off from the reality of the new country. We cannot be reduced, or tempted to reduce ourselves, to being foreigners only. First of all we are individuals; we must also be observers and thinkers. Good writers are also good psychologists, able to speak to their new readers not only through the prism of foreigner-protagonist, but also from the reader's perspective.

Milan Kundera emigrated to France from Czechoslovakia. Until 1984 all his novels took place in his homeland, but since then he has developed a more cosmopolitan voice. He rebelled against being reduced to 'writer in exile' or 'writer-dissident', demanding for himself the broader recognition he deserves as an international writer –philosopher and defender of individualism. Bharati Mukherjee was told in the 70s by American publishers and critics that the only way for her to succeed as a writer would be to describe Calcutta's upper-class exotica. She obeyed for a while and the price she paid, as she states in one of her essays, was to become a part of the mainstream writing. Eventually she rebelled and developed her own voice, writing novels about American reality.

In *Lolita* Nabokov described 1950s America as no one else – through a European foreigner's eyes. Using his 'outsider' identity, and enriched by his life in different parts of Europe and America, Nabokov served Americans up their own paradoxical melange of sweet naiveté and vulgarity with a new dressing. He didn't limit himself to one language either, publishing books in Russian and English. Moreover, while living in Europe during the 1920s and 1930s Nabokov wrote a few short stories in French. Critics regarded him as a literary anomaly, a foreign genius somehow working accidentally in both the Russian and English languages. Ilan Stavans, a Professor of Latino studies at Amherst College and a notable writer, said that there are writers who overcome being from one country. He is a bilingual writer who was born in Mexico to Eastern-European Jewish parents and now lives in America. He says: "I write in English for Americans about topics they know little about, and I write in Spanish to Mexicans … I act as a bridge, I symbolise dialogue."

My multiple identities used to be a burden. My early 20s were spent trying to reduce and simplify my biography while developing my own fictional voice. I was afraid of confusing readers, but also myself. However, while observing different aspects of life I started to accept the parallel between them and my complex identity, different occupations, names, languages, lovers, and beliefs. The same process applies to writing, which behaves like the human brain during adolescence: creating more intricate connections, and paths form between its neurons, making it more and more complex. One reason Scottish Gaels have been *so* successful in almost every field is almost certainly the intellectual flexibility which stems from their being bilingual. Every day I learn more about how to benefit from this complexity, but still have a long way to go. V S Naipaul describes people like us as being "of no tribe". The image that comes to mind is of a ghost floating between different dimensions. Perhaps this is melodramatic, but I like the weightlessness and freedom of this image. It is refreshing after the gravity of communist parades, the religious rituals of my childhood home and the Israeli army service of my youth. There is always guilt about being the observer, the uprooted wanderer, but there is something very human at its core. Stripped of a country of origin, a mother tongue and a clear sense of belonging, what remains is a bare humanity which enables you to relate to each individual you encounter. Is this the significance of the writer-immigrant's voice?

And the wise man said to the confused immigrant-writer: "Now that you have defeated the three-headed hydra, I have news for you. Unfortunately I did not study Greek mythology thoroughly. It appears that this lovely water snake has been variously reputed to have nine, or fifty, or one hundred heads. So I am sorry, but you'll have to go back and fight.

(Based on Brewer's Concise Phrase & Fable)

Barbara Cormack (1938-2004)

I Thought You'd Like to Know

It's safe now
to let me put milk bottles out
last thing at night.
Nowadays the light
is stronger than the beckoning dark. Time was
you might have lost me
to it. Did you know?

Nightly tempted at the secret brink,
I used to think
of others similarly bending
and of the clink of bottles dominoing
round in secret chains of sound,
the prisoners sending through the air
soft signals of despair.

Time was
I might have been
the queen of rural bag ladies, living rough,
growing old, tricked out
in rags and plastic bags; time was
nearly ticked out
inside my head.

That's what babies do.
They make
the streets at night unsafe
for new-born mothers. Babies take
and take and take and take and
slaked at last they sleep. The weary mothers,
washing up plates, put away their selves
upon the shelves,
and last of all
put out the empty bottles.

That's the danger time,
that's when you have to call us to the light,
that's
when we may turn and return from the night,
or else decide to go
into the undemanding dark
of the cold hedgerow.

From Greenland's Icy Mountains

Cold of my childhood, chilling still!
Night cold, the solitary sentinel
in the dark window willed
the passing beams to swing
window-way, turn at the turning; bring
something, some one,
some turning towards, some
message from the world.
Always they swept on
to other assignations,
raking bedroom walls and eager face
with the brief excitement of their leopard light,
light and life elsewhere bound.

Cold of my childhood, chilling still!
And still it is the solitary heart that swings
into the traffic's stream: watchful, apart,
skilled in spycraft, camouflage and guile:
how to smile,
how to strike from sparks of ice
holograms of fire.

Cold of my fathers, killing still,
blight cold! Renunciation cannot will
away the legacy of permafrosted hours,
though poems bloom
like tundra flowers.

Landscape with Tree

I wonder if
someone else will see
the berries on this hawthorn tree?
Green now, they will burn
beacon bright, like the rowan's
come October.
I shall have gone south by then,
and the shepherds will have done
with shearing, so there will be none
to pass this cottage
and remark the tree.
Oh, it could be men will come to mend
the coal shed door,
or some late walker tramp to the loch's end.

I should like to think some friend
will pass this way and look into the clearing
before the hawthorn has itself
gone for shearing.

Looking Back

Don't look back. You made
the incredible jump from bed to rug;
the witches snatched
but couldn't quite catch
your ankles. The wicker chair *nearly* got you ...
Well, the thing you would have seen
had you been
so silly as to look at the wicker chair ...
There's a piece of luck!
The thing to remember now
is don't look back. Stare
at the kitchen door at the end of the passage
where the light falls.
Walk slowly
and don't look back

If you look sideways a little
(not too much: don't lose sight of the light)
there's a hole in the plaster
where once you woke from sleep
to find yourself searching with curious fingers
for dream butterflies. But don't look
up. Up is dangerous. The stain
where the rain came in last November becomes Baba Yaga.
And don't look back. Black
is behind you, waiting to wind you,
with sharp green, bony hands,
into the dark.

By day, they'll say (when you've turned the corner
into the blinding temporary safety of the kitchen),
you'll see that the wicker chair always adjusts its bones
and groans for no good reason,
that the Baba Yagas underneath the bed
are only in your head.
Look! Look and see, they'll say. I may.
But I won't look now,
and it won't be day
until tomorrow.

New Year

The winter sun cannot clear the holly
(how it has grown since first we came!).
Shutters scarce opened
close on my morning heart:
no more downstairs sun today,
now just the chilling of the light,
foreknowledge of the coming of the winter's night.

Across the way windows flame red,
catch day; one imagines glowing rooms within.
It is twilight here in the shadow of the holly,
in the shadow
of the valley of the shadow.

There Is That

There is that which longs to be
free even from love, that sends the eye
to the top twig of a high hill's tree
and higher still, then
to the sky, as if perfection with unmoving wings
hovered on ethers, never plummeting
to the untidy kill.

Martin Cook
Barbara Cormack

I think of Frost's birches
look out of the window and see
one that has delighted me;
tall, elegant and dressed with fresh leaves,
as it gestures in the wind as though blessing.

There is strength and fragility
in the tree's soft movements,
and I think of the delicacy of Red Admirals
that will arrive with buddleia's mauve
to remind me of the Cherokee legend:

how spirits of the dead return
as butterflies to reassure loved ones,
and to implant in their hearts
hope and wonderful memories
of what they had given.

Cheese
Roy Kesey

Redeemed and thus liberated – Carlo Ginzburg, *The Cheese and the Worms*

It would appear that in the previous interrogation you contradicted yourself in regard to the provenance of the angels. Therefore clarify this circumstance and your belief.

Back to that again, are we? Once more: earth and air and water and fire were mixed together, and out of that bulk a mass was formed, the way cheese forms in milk. Worms appeared in the mass, and those worms, once blessed by God with will, intellect and memory, were the angels.

As if out of cheese, then?

So to speak.

Are we talking the whole celestial hierarchy here, or –?

No. Archangels, and angels properly speaking.

Whence then the others? The principalities and powers?

As if out of butter.

The virtues, dominions and thrones?

Out of yogurt.

The cherubim? The seraphim?

Whipped cream and meringue, respectively.

I will have you know that meringue is not a dairy product.

Is that my problem?

Not your biggest one.

Which is?

That the Holy Roman Office of the Inquisition has charged you with twisting maliciously, affirming diabolically, and contriving wickedly, with persevering obdurately, with causing to resurface and asserting as true the ancient philosopher's censured opinion that there was an eternal chaos from which originated everything of this world, and with resurrecting the Manichaean doctrine of the dual generation of good and evil, thereby putting at risk the entire Counter-Reformation program as such.

All on account of the meringue?

Hardly. You –

Because I'd be willing to reconsider as far as the meringue goes.

You know perfectly well that meringue is but the beginning, and may I remind you that should said charges be judged true, you would be obliged to abjure your heresies publicly, to fulfil various unpleasant salutary penances, and to spend the rest of your life in prison wearing nothing but a *habitello*. Does that sound like a laughing matter to you?

The *habitello* sounds a little funny.

It is, a little.

Right. Next question?

Have you any knowledge of the future?

A tiny bit. Minimal. More sort of a presentiment than anything else.
Namely?
That it ends badly.
Badly is hardly the word.
Really?
I'm so very sorry. I cannot, however, allow my sorrow to change things.
Of course not.
I have a job to perform. Don't think this is easy for me.
I would never think such a thing.
Because –
It's okay. I understand. Go ahead, ask the next question.
Right. Sorry, I just ... OK. Who are your accomplices? Your disciples? Your hangers-on?
Um. Counting Melchiorre Gerbas?
Melchiore the Moron?
The very same.
Poor bastard. No, we'll deal with him later. Right now we're more interested in movers, shakers, folks that could be dangerous if your ideas took hold.
In that case, none that I know of. Pretty much everyone here in the greater Friuli area thinks I'm kind of a ding-dong, religion-wise.
And yet there's no way a simple miller such as yourself could have come up with all these ideas.
There were the books.
Right, the books. Let's see, Boccaccio, Mandeville, the Bible, *Il Fioretto* ... Nope, no dice, still too many loose ends. Names and addresses of everybody you've ever spoken with, if you'd be so kind. .
You know I can't tell you.
And you know what happens if you don't.
Torture?
Bull's-eye.
I ... Damn. Sorry, no can do.
Fine. Take that!
Ow! Never!
And that!
Ow! Francesco Montareale!
OK, I think that about does it for now.
What's that supposed to mean?
That you will indeed be condemned as a heretic and heresiarch, and will be obliged to recite your abjuration, candle in hand, at the entrance to the cathedral; that during your two years here in this dark dank prison you will pray often, fast on Fridays, and seem most truly repentant; that in a letter to Fra Evangelista Paleo you will recant, beg forgiveness and mercy, and promise never again to fall into error; that you will gain a hearing, and at said hearing will weep and plead and prostrate yourself;

that you will then be released, and resume to a certain extent your place in the community; and that at some later point you will start spreading your filthy lies yet again, will again be arrested and tried, will be condemned as a recidivist, and at the age of sixty-seven, on the direct order of Pope Clement VII, will be led to and burned at the stake.

Really?

That's what it says here.

Let's have a look ... Wow. Well, if that's what it says ...

Yes.

Hold on. According to this, I don't get tortured until my second trial, fifteen years from now.

We've tried to follow the spirit of the thing rather than the letter.

But you're getting the essentials?

Each and every one.

So you're saying this is it?

Pretty much. See you in 1599?

OK. No, wait, hold on, don't, don't go just yet.

Yes?

And afterwards?

Afterwards when?

Once I'm gone for good. Does anything come of it?

You mean does anything come of your ideas and suffering and ignominious, horrifying death?

Yes.

Well ... OK. I mean, I'm not supposed to, but, well, OK. Yes, something comes of it. After it's done, after you're gone, there will be a rumour, third-hand at best, that a peasant here in the Friuli has been heard saying that when the body dies, the soul dies too.

That's it? One lousy theosophical descendent?

Sorry.

Well. What's his name?

Marco, or Marcato. The record won't be clear.

And what becomes of him?

Nothing, as far as we know.

No massive uprising, no revolution ...

Nope.

How depressing.

Yes. But there's something else as well. This book itself.

What about it?

Posterity. Those who come later will want to know certain things, and this book will tell them, and without you there would be no book.

Things like what?

Like the manner in which one might use discrepancies attributable neither to suggestive questioning nor to torture between my questions and your replies to expose the filter that you interposed unconsciously between yourself and the texts you've read, said filter presupposing an oral culture composed partly of autonomous but obscure peasant mythologies that might well serve as evidence of a millenarian cosmological tradition, said mythologies having later been grafted onto a complex of ideas ranging from a naturalism that tended toward the scientific to utopian aspirations of social reform.

Interesting.

Very. Also, and I'm sure you'll agree this is a good thing, it will hypothesise meaningfully in regard to reciprocal influences between the dominant classes on one hand and the subordinate classes on the other, and will use your case, lacking in macro-historical significance, and representative by virtue of that lack, to demonstrate the extent to which one might exercise one's conditional liberty within the not-altogether inflexible cage formed of the latent possibilities of a peasant culture otherwise known only through fragmentary, distorted documents from the very archives of those who sought to repress said culture.

Will anyone read this book?

Mostly historians and their students.

Not promising.

No, but there will be others. A few others. A handful.

Enough?

For what?

Fair question. Although …

What?

I was just thinking. Maybe there's some way around all this.

A way to beat the book?

Exactly.

None that I know of. You could always try, of course. But bear in mind what you'd be risking.

Marco, or Marcato.

And the existence of the text itself.

Damn.

Yup.

So.

So.

I guess you'd better be off, then.

I guess so.

Take care.

You too.

Write when you can.

I will if you will.

You know I will.

And you know I will.

OK then.

OK.

Alexis Lykiard

Colour Theories

The one unanswerable question – what is Blue?
Blue's invisibility becoming visible,
belongs transparently to me – retorts the shade of Klein:
you opt for the abyss, embrace the sky's true emptiness
placing all emphasis on unambiguous utterance.
Space without borders may reflect sublimity. The fine
Idea remains, dispelling more romantic formulae

or mirrors of our mortal selves ... Ultramarine?
An impure mixture, not a global trademark-hue!
Poor Lowry's brain distilled a lurid brew: he
hoped to reproduce long-faded siren-songs,
but any new tone founders on a tide of blues.
When plain nostalgia reigns, wipes out coherence,
it sounds a silence incorruptibly sea-green.

Interim Gob

Les Pères de l'Eglise, eux, ils connaissaient leur boulot. Ils promettaient le bonheur mais pour l'autre monde (Céline, Mea Culpa, 1936)

Call yourself an atheist, surrealist?
Call yourself a raver?
Do us a favour
at the very least
while your spirits are merry
yet quite sober & unpissed
do it in remembrance of Péret
do it today
Spit on a priest!
Nothing odd
gobbing gofers for a god
who in his (lower) case
never merits CAPS.
Titles being a bourgeois lapse,
our Nameless Abject Concept's
neither here nor there
nor any otherwhere
so, spit right at 'its' face
hanging out in space!
Some ancient with a cloudy beard
foams at the mouth and rains down weird?

Don't relent in any case:
it pleased one playwright to insist
the bastard doesn't exist.
Get on with the show,
let honest phlegm flow!
Summon your oyster, mister,
and you do likewise, sister!
Are you cretins? Are you cattle?
Then let's hear that spittle rattle!
Go on, go gob a priest!
Now god's gone East
(gone gaga, missing, feared deceased)
we'll need extremer deeds not words, at least,
to dump an outworn myth without a function.
Unleash, therefore, your salivary unction
for it's high time to hawk at the religionist.
Respond to the call, let fly at them all!
It won't hurt at all,
so join in the gobfest and spit on a priest!

David Gascoyne told me Péret interrupted their chat on a bus to spit at a seated curé – the surrealist's daily ritual observance.

A Sign (Outside Christian Science Reading Room)

BOOKS CASSETTES AND CDs ON SPIRITUALITY FOR SALE
Unpunctuated! So it's clear all these
enticements spell out ambiguity.
One passing cynic smiles – here's small concern
if market forces wholly rule. We learn
how, showing their bold assiduity,
religionists set out to bait and tease:
by soulful prostitution, sure to please,
a groping mind may buy its piece of tail.

Rabbi Dismembered by Rent Boy
(Guardian headline 15.09.04)

It happens, shit happens, Oy Vey!
Yet whether you're young or you pray,
God gets you – you pay anyway.
Believer or not, one is too soon destroyed,
so if you're devout and rabbinically Out,
drink not with strange goy (tattooed, unemployed),
for none can avoid picking up on The Void.
Nice boys deserve favour, they say:
Jahweh may choose you, if you're gay.

Further Theological Speculations (21.09.04)
Religionists awake, bow to Sod's Law, at least!
The holy pervert vows (ditto the arsy priest):
"No shame, hellfire or risk shall discompose my feast."
But they are fair game too, who bait the human beast.

"Taking Drugs Seriously"
(Sale rack, Exeter Central Library, June 2003)

NB, book-title and a half,
provocative in various ways,
oddity, puzzlement or laugh –
vexed theme and treatment, to amaze
the reader or librarian here.
How else should drugs be taken? Lots of choice for one and all:
drink, sex, opiate. Prescriptions by the likes of St Paul.

Drugs recreational, for kicks,
are fun. Others alleviate
all sorts of ills, as desperate
measures. A medicinal fix
may heal the pain and calm the fear.
This dull tome's peddled for pence – its worthy tone leaves us cold.
Buy such stuff and you must want brains and substances controlled.

Curmudgeonly Haiku

1: An Agnostic Aesthete
Larkin: "The Bible's
a load of balls of course, but
very beautiful."

2: An Anglican Atheist
P.L.: "I am not
somebody who lost his faith.
I never had it."

3: Unrequired Writing (or, Trouble at Willow Gables)
Dorm, with Larkin dykes:
truth amid the alien porn
tastes of youth turned sour.

The God Couple

They make a pretty devout Christian pair,
brainless Gee Bush and bleeding-heart Tee Blare.

Only Dead Fish Swim with the Flow
Sheila Mullen

I was born Sheila Elizabeth Speed on 24th January 1942 in Glasgow (looking at my influences, I should have hung off for a day). The subsequent war years were spent on the family farm near Auchtermuchty in Fife. Returning to Glasgow I attended Bankhead Primary and Hilhead High School. Went to Jean Irwin's Art classes in Kelvingrove Art Gallery from about 1950-59 but didn't learn much, and turned up at Glasgow School of Art artistically virgin, not surprising given that the family were totally uncultured and heavily Presbyterian. Life began to get better when I met and married Sam Mullen in 1962 – and am still heavily married to him …

Despite being diagnosed with multiple sclerosis in 1963, against medical advice I had four children – and it whacked the MS. Didn't paint for 12 years but turned to making cloth hangings, sculptures, toys, clothes etc. When child four was about 4 I started painting, ever a late unpredictablility. Landscapes, seascapes, treescapes, plainscapes, riverscapes always a draw, I moved to Sandbank, Argyll in 1972 then Johnstonebridge in 1977 and started painting 'properly'. First exhibition Carlisle art school, then Paris by invitation. For rest, Cee Vee!

I always loved the Ballads and even as a teenager warbled away at folk-songs, and my brush is still involuntarily pushed by the rich, earthy sounds of the Scots tongue. I've painted the twa corbies; Leda and the Swan; El Çid (Scots is international); Susannah and the Elders; etc at Art School. Make of this what you will, but I paint in Scots!

I always went out to paint. Everything was tied on to my bike, me, water bottle, comestibles, paint-brushes – and large canvasses. In 1992 we moved to our present house, farm, steading and land, and I could increase my agglomeration of animals – sheep, cows, cats, dogs, tortoises. I've always loved everything to do with life, and it broke my heart when the stock was all destroyed contiguosly culling due to foot and mouth in 2001. One blow leads to another, and I managed to fall off the roof while painting the house the same year. Clever girl: I smashed my right elbow and suffered deep concussion, losing my sight for 2 months.

Maybe the grim reaper is feared at me. He gets his chance, his 'in', as with the MS, but through whatever drives me, I jink away. Then there was the fall, but the shock of the injury, the blindness, which only intensified the inner eye, so I kept painting – you can put a good gal down, but not out. The Erlkönig might be chasing me, but I was blinded by the light of all those sights and sounds erupting out of my palette. To those who are twice, or even thrice reborn, time takes on a different hue; you become aware of allotted spans, but also somehow untouchable, immortal. It takes a lot to shuffle you off your mortals if that reborn spirit dominates. Ye cannae stap a burn in spate! I started series of paintings around songs and poems: auld sangs, Burns, MacDiarmid, Hogg, the Bible, songs, anything that made my heart purr and the inner eye shine.

I've always had a passion for Scotland – its landscape, history, and culture. I've tried to become a part of the landscape, live in it, surrounded by greens, blues, whites, browns – and all the other myriad colours nature 'subjects' us to. I realised that so may people, long before me, have felt the same, laughed and cried, loved and hated, just as I did. So the Border Ballads began to take shape on my canvasses, the stories unleashing themselves from a dictated brush.

Border Ballads! Frontier spirit! All those marches, the horses with open, snorting nostrils! And the riders canny chiels. This soil was blood-soaked. There must be hundreds of murder-sites, burial places of knights, their dames, and babies. I've painted *The Cruel Mother* many times, feeling especially for the woman, knowing she munna loe the babe she wis carryin: "smile nae sae sweet my bonnie babe, an ye smile sae sweet, ye'll smile me dear". I love the economy of the ballads, which say and imply so much with so few words. Tried to paint in same way – saying a lot with little detail. Painting *Clerk Saunders and May Margaret* I was astonished at the cruelty and tenderness. Drama or what!

The ballads rise the hair on my neck, the tears never faur awa. *The Battle of Otterburn* is fu o the chaos o battle, the only calm creatures, the cheviots, watching frae the hill. I feel so much magic in the countryside linking me to long-ago people and events. MacDiarmid has become a favourite (near neighbour in Langholm Post Office) and I've painted *Crowdieknowe* several times. The *Lang Deed* didnae want roused so I've made the angels play a jazzy last trump and put God in a cheerfu red dress. And e'en that'll nae pit fear intae thae men wi tousled beards!

Burns says in words what I've often painted: his landscape, corn-rigs, barley rigs, sweet Aftons, and lots of flesh, tits and bums. I'm not afraid of the great elementals, and happy to piggy-back on those who have made it alive in words. I copy and interpret in paint, bunnet on the grund. I've gone back to Celtic themes with the Horned God and Sheela-na-Gig, sexy earth mother, complete with pussy. Gaelic songs like Heart of Firelove and Scots ones like The Great Selkie are a great source. The Bible: the poetry and cruelty of the creation myth – *The Creation* several times, Adam 'in', Eve 'oot', and whit aboot thae puir barns, scars an aa. Then there's the flood: Noah, Susannah and the Elders, Jesus entering Jerusalem, the Nativity, where the baby is surrounded by animals, sheep and cows, because he liked their warm, aromatic, moist, sweet breaths.

Through the MS, the fall, the blindness, my sight is sharper and my will more focused. Even 'terminal illnesses' cannot stop the flow. Live fish swim, tide or nae tide! Live fish swim where they must.

Sheila Mullen

Self Portrait (1962)

Only Dead Fish Swim with the Flow (2005)

Schiehallion (2002)

Callanish (2004)

The Great Silkie (2005)

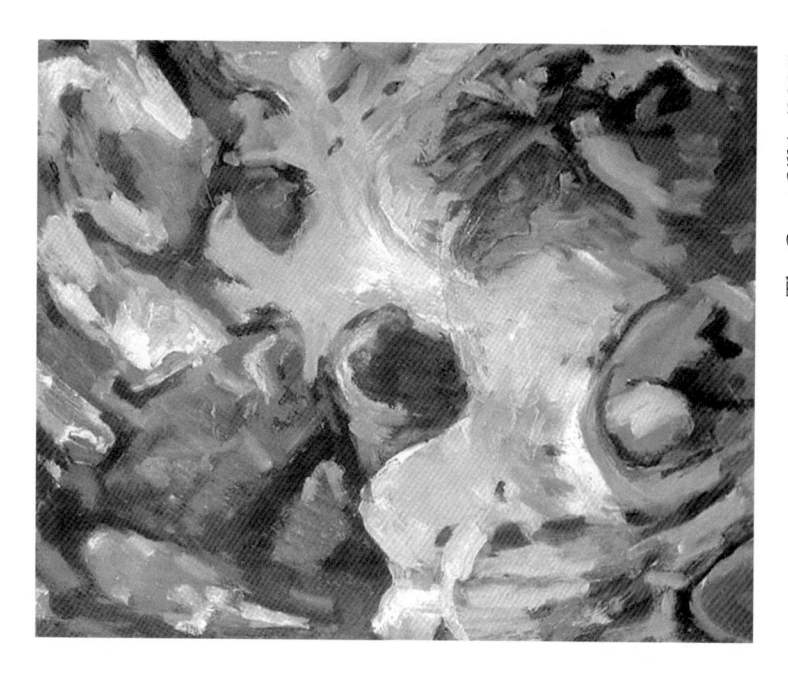

Martinwhat Rig (2) (1980)

Horned God (2004)

Tam Linn (2003)

King Orpheus (2004)

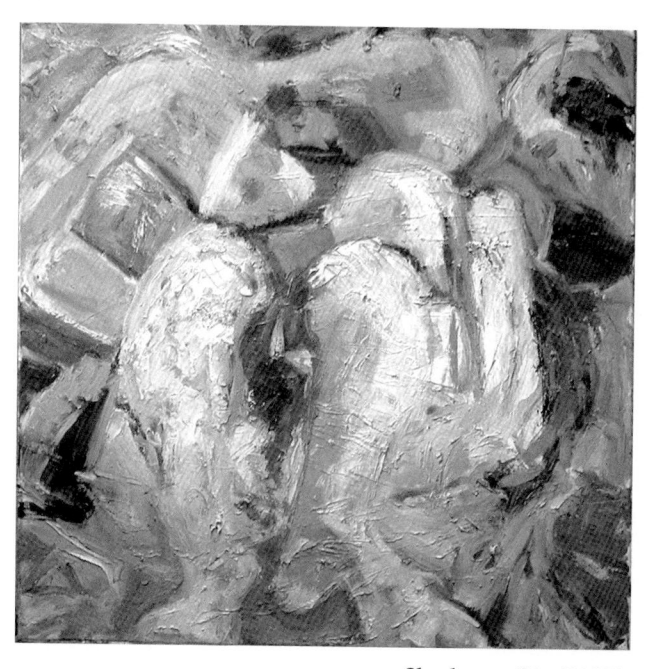

Sheela-na-Gig (2005)

Scaurhead (3) (1979)

River Dee at Dildawn (2001)

Dildown, Tim's Pond (2001)

Sir Patrick Spens (2004)

Adam and Eve (2005)

Caroline's Cow (2004)

VisitSheilaMullen'swebsite:www.sheilamullen.co.uk

End of the Rainbow
Ruth Atkinson

I found the pot of gold. It was sitting there right where it should have been. A big clay pot full of coins. Not all gold, mind. Mostly silver in fact but there were some gold ones, wrapped up in a cloth right at the bottom of the pot. I couldn't believe it. It was sitting there, right in the middle of a muddy field.

Well I took it, didn't I? I had to dig a bit, scraping away with my hands. But it was easy enough to get it out of the ground. Finders keepers, eh? I took it home, back to the van. Stuck it on the table and stared at it. I think I must have gone a bit doolally for a while. All I could do was stare. If I didn't stare I got to laughing so's I couldn't stop. That scared me. I'd never had luck like that before.

Then she came. Well, she would wouldn't she? Always turning up like a bad penny, especially then, just when I had all those good pennies. The best bloody pennies I'd ever had, or ever likely to have.

She worried about me she said. She should have been worried with me sitting there laughing my head off. She gave me such a fright when she turned up. Poking about in the yard, setting Jimmy's mutt to barking. I picked up my old knife, the one I use for skinning rabbits after I've been on the prowl. She knocked on the door. At least she knocked. Oftentimes she just barges straight in. Well that gave me time to think a little. I shoved the pot in the sink along with the dirty washing and stuck the knife back in my old bag where it belonged. I was all smiles when I opened the door. No wonder she was suspicious.

"What've you been up to Ned?" she asked.

"You're not usually so cheerful. Have you won the lottery?"

Trust her; straight to the point. Sticking her nose in where it's not wanted. Well I didn't say anything to that. I just stopped smiling and told her to fuck off. That usually shuts her up for a bit. Doesn't get rid of her though. I'd have to get the knife out, but that would just lead to trouble.

She wanted a cup of tea. Said she hadn't seen me for a while and needed to catch up, see how I was doing. I couldn't be having that. She might see the pot in the sink when she went to fill the kettle. I said I had no matches for the stove. She wouldn't have believed me. I've always got a light for my rollies but she couldn't search me, could she? She wouldn't want to either I'm sure. Not the state I'm in. I haven't had a woman within three feet of me for a good while. Not since I was in the hospital that time, and they turned their noses up then too.

Then she started poking about in the 'van. Opening the cupboards and tut-tutting. Not that she found anything. I don't keep much about me. The odd rabbit for the pot and some greens from the hedge and spuds from the field, that's the only decent meal for me. Fags and whisky keep me going the rest of the time and old Jimmy sometimes comes in after the pub with a bag of chips to stretch the booze a bit further. She put some tins in the cupboard, beans and stuff. Healthy she says, but I know what keeps me healthy and it's not beans. It smells bad enough in here without bean farts to add to it all.

I could see the pot in the sink. Sitting there like a great fat Buddha. One of the hippies down the road had one of those. I saw it one day when I was feeling good and felt like a bit of a chinwag. He asked me in for a smoke and it was sitting right next to his fireplace, half-naked with his big belly sticking out in front of him. The hippie said the Buddha was enlightened, that's why he didn't care about his fat belly. He was light enough. I liked that, I'd like to be light enough, like the Buddha. But all I've got is the belly, and even that's not up to much.

The rain had washed the mud off the pot and its pink belly spread over my greasy plates like a baby, sitting in its dirty nappies. It looked satisfied, like the Buddha does or babies do after they've filled a nappy. You couldn't miss it. Not even she could miss it. She saw it when she shut the cupboard and started looking for something else to stick her nose into. "That's a funny looking pot Ned," she said, pointing to my sink.

"It looks really old. I've seen pots like that in the museum. Did someone give it to you?"

That's just like her, never gives me credit for anything.

"I bloody found it, didn't I?"

I couldn't let her get away with that, assuming things. She did it all the time, thinking she knew me. She knows nothing about me. Just because Social Services have a file on me, she thought it was gospel. The gospel of Ned, full of damned good stories. There's a good few more but I'm not letting on to them about everything. If they haven't found it out for themselves I'm not going to help them.

"I know the archaeologist at the museum. He might come and have a look at it for you. You know what an archaeologist is, don't you Ned? Someone who studies old things."

There she goes again. Of course I know what an archaeologist is, ancient-bloody-ologist. Oh, I'm not ignorant, not like she thinks I am. I've read a few books in my time, even thought about studying. But she wouldn't believe that of me. Good few years back mind. Back when I thought I liked people, some people anyway.

She went, at last. It took her a while though. She kept going on about the archaeologist, how he'd like to meet me. I bet he would. At least he'd recognise an ancient monument if he saw me. But what would he see in the pot? I couldn't let him see that, not here. Precious things, even dirty precious things, don't belong here. He'd want to take it away from me. I wasn't going to let him do that. If he wanted the pot he'd have to find it.

So I took it back. I dug a little hole and dropped it in. The pot broke and the coins spilled into the mud, glinting in the rain. I knelt there for a while. There was no rainbow then. My coat kept the rain off for a while but then it started running down my back, cutting channels through the dirt and chilling me to my old bones. I scrabbled about in the hole, groping about for a coin to keep. My fingers were all thumbs in the wet and I couldn't get hold of one at first. I managed at last. It was that small I could barely feel it between my old sausages. But it was there, shining up at me with a picture of some dead king on it. I couldn't make out what was on the other side. It looked like one of those old gods, half-man half-creature that I used to read about. I put it in my pocket. It was all I needed for now. One at a time, that's the best way to do it. I know where it is, which is more than that smart-arse archaeologist. I can always come back.

Sheila Mullen – *Broch*

John Law

Haein a news wi ye
Owreset frae Pablo Neruda's Explico Algunas Cosas

Awa ti speir – an whaur's aa the lilacs?
an the metaphysics clartit wi poppies?
An the onding dirlin oot
his words ti pirlicue them
wi insichts an wi birds?

Lat's hae a news, hae aa ma news thegither.

I bade in a barrio o Madrid,
Madrid o the bells
o the clocks, o the trees.

Thonner awa we leukit oot
atour Castile's cabbrach pow
lik a seascape o ledder.
                    Ma hoose wis cried
hoose o the flouers sen aagates
geraniums fair explodit: it wis
a bonnie hoose
wi dugs an weans.
                    Raoul, mynd?
Dae you mynd, Rafael?
                    Federico, dae you mynd
frae unner mools
mynd ma hoose wi the balconies
whaur the licht o June stappit flouers in yer mou?
                            Brither, ma brither!

Aathing wis
lood vyces, sautit troke,
bings o pipperin breid
mercat staas o the Arguelles bit I bade, wi thon statue
lik a tuim inkwal amang hake-fish:
olive ile trintelt on the spuins,
a deep dirlin
o hauns an feet fuhled the gate,
metres, litres, the eident
smeddum o life,
            fishes fair stoukit,
ruiftaps waft unner a cauld sun
whaur the cocksails ar trauchelt,

a braw wuidness o ivory tatties,
tomaitas rowein doun til the sea.

An ae mornin aa this wis ableize
an ae mornin banefires
brust frae the yirth,
burnin awa lifes,
an sinsyne fire,
gunpouther sinsyne,
an sinsyne bluid.
Reivers wi planes an wi Moors,
reivers wi fingir-rings an duchesses
reivers wi black friars' blissins
rade frae the luft ti kill weans,
an oot on the gate the bluid o the weans
fair ran free, as weans' bluid will.

Jackals the jackal wadna awn them,
stanes the thrawn thristle ruit wad bite an gob,
edders edders sels wad cowk at.

I hae seen the bluid o Spain
rise up fornent ye,
ti droun ye in ae spate
o pride an blades!

Traitor
generals:
see whit deid ma hoose is,
leuk at the wrack o Spain:
but frae ilka deid hoose airn rins afire
insteid o flouers,
frae ilka shell-howe in Spain
Spain seeds,
frae ilka deid wean a gun wi een,
ilk crime is faither o buhlets
that ae day yit will seek oot
yer hert.

Aye want ti ken whit wey his poems
disna tell us o his dreams, an leafs,
an muckle volcanoes in his mitherland?

Come an see the bluid in the streets,
come an see
the bluid in the streets,
come an see the bluid
in the streets!

Hallaig

(Owreset frae Somhairle mac Gille-Eain)

"The deer, time, liggs in Hallaig shaw."

The windae's nailt an broddit up
whaur-throu I saw the airt o the Wast
an ma luve is at the burn o Hallaig
in her bunnet o birk, an she wis aye

atween Inver an Mulkie Linn
thare or thareaboots roun Baile-Chuirn wey,
cled in a birk, in a hazel,
in a young rowan straucht an sclender.

In Screapadal whaur ma ain fowk wis,
whaur Norman an Big Hector bade,
thair dochters an thair sons is a wid
raxin up alang the burnside.

Prood the nicht the pine cocks
craws on the heicht o Cnoc an Ra
straucht thair spaulds in the muinlicht –
no thaim the wids o ma hert.

I will byde on the birken shaw
whit time it raxes til the Cairn
whit lenth the haill rig til its scadda
owre Ben na Lice dis lour.

Gin it disna, I'm awa doun til Hallaig
til the sabbath o the deid
wi aa the fowk in thrangity
ilk generation that's awa.

Thay'r aa aye in Hallaig
MacLeans an MacLeods
aa thaim thare frae MacGille Chaluim's day:
the deid haes been seen, leivin yit –

the menfowk lyin on the gress
ilk gavel-en o ilka hoose that's been,
the lassies a wid o birk trees,
straucht thair spaulds, blate thair heids.

Atween the Leac an Fearns
a braird o moss saftens the hie road
an the lassies in seilent bauns thegither
gangs til Clachan as frae the first.

An comin back frae Clachan,
frae Suisnish an the land o the leivin –
ilkane young an licht o fuit
wi nae hertbrek in the story.

Burn o Fearns lenth o sea-tint cladach
sae clair in the raivelment o the hills
the'r nocht but thon congregation o the lassies
aye haudin forrit at thair endless haik,

returnin til Hallaig come the eenin
in the dumb leivin gloamin
fuhlin the stey braes
thair lauchter in ma listenin lik a haar

thair fairheid watterin ma hert's een
gin comes the mirk owre the kyles,
gin gangs the sun the back o Dun Cana
a buhlet frae luve's gun will come threipin

an stote thon deer that gangs stoiterin
snowkin at the gressy larachs;
he will faa in the wid, his ee jeelin;
whyle I live, ye winna finnd his bluid.

'The Corrie' Sailin
(Owreset frae Siubhal a' Choire, bi George Campbell Hay)

Up an awa oot wi us on the green sea machairs liftit
an we pit past dour Garvel o the gurlin storms –
lowps on us syne a sair blast wast bi sooth, an hard rain.
Up wi her heid, prow fornent cauld wave-heids
stoondin an stunnin, a slim dark lassie,
up wi her sang an surgin forrit.

She streikit her lee sheet ticht as steel
she streikit her hainch til the thies o the brekkers
she streikit her gait til the gait o the ocean
she gaed dunt wi her gunnel gin yaw
an dunt wi the seam o her shouther gaed she
an ryvit the wave wi her beak at the pitch.

Come Eilean Aoidh she raired oot joyfu
Ardlamont haerd her prood bellin
bi Inchmarnock she crooned a douce air.
Oorsels wappit in her smeik – smoorit-nane –
that stang in oor een frae the ram-stam o her
in a spelder o speindrift an saut spray
an nocht cuid we hear but the pulse o her pechin.

Trying to Make My Hideous Progeny Walk
Louise Welsh

When I was about ten years old I found an old accountancy book at my granddad's house. It had sombre grey cover, watered endpapers and its pages were empty except for a few incomprehensible markings in brown copperplate. My granddad had been a clerk of works for Edinburgh City Corporation and I suppose the book had somehow found its way into the house via his job. I thought the book looked sad, junked away in amongst the old bits and pieces we were allowed to rifle through and so I rescued it from its empty existence and turned it into my confidant.

This first effort at writing held intimations of later sufferings. My handwriting wasn't nearly distinguished enough for the fine red and green ruled pages of the grand volume and my frustrations with school life and annoying parents lost their power written down. But despite the suspicion that the book would rather have been left amongst the detritus of my granddad's spare room until someone worthier than me came along to fill it I persisted, writing my journal most nights and illustrating my entries with drawings in felt tip. Like Adrian Mole's my diary was a well-kept secret. I hid it beside my other treasures under a dodgy floorboard in the room I shared with my sister. I wrote in it for about a year and then when the book was full I stopped. Perhaps the project had been less about recording my life than finding a use for the swanky old tome.

My snooty confidant is long since lost, probably still hiding under the floor of the council flat I left over twenty years ago. And though I'm a great fan of other people's diaries, I've never kept one of my own again. I find writing my own life fills me with an urge to self-harm. So this account of my time in Grez-sur-Loing won't be a chronicle of emotions, drunkenness, drug abuse, sexual exploits or self-discovery. And even though there's an interesting tale to be told in how one of my fellow artists fell in love with and was betrayed by another resident, Sweden's own Peter Pan of pop, writing it here would be a second betrayal.

So instead I'm going to recount how I didn't do what I intended to do when I was given two months' writing time at the Hôtel Chévillon, but how I did come up with something else.

The hotel is run by the Swedish Cultural Institute who give several residencies to Swedish artists and also rent out rooms to their Finnish equivalent and to The National Library of Scotland who administer the Robert Louis Stevenson Award enabling a few fortunate Scottish writers to go to the hotel for two months of uninterrupted writing. In the summer of 2002 I was lucky enough to be granted one of the awards and headed off with a song in my heart and a French/English dictionary in my bag.

My intention was to crack the novel I was working on. It was called

Torchlight and 40,000 words of it are still stored on the same laptop I'm writing this on now. The novel had grown out of a short story called 'Private View' about an usherette called Carol who would rather have been an actress, but had missed her moment and now spent her days showing punters to their seats in a crumbling movie theatre. It's not in my nature to keep things quiet and introspective so the story also featured a slimy cinema manager who it transpired was director of his own wee movie, starring Carol and recorded without her knowledge as she got changed into her uniform prior to the evening show. The crux of the story was that Carol was destroyed not just by the knowledge that her boss had been videoing her in her undies, but how bad she looked in the film.

Perhaps 'Private View' was partly based on a friend, lets call her Camilla, who'd let a boyfriend snap some sexy photos of her but regretted it when long after they'd split she heard he'd been showing them to his drinking buddies. Camilla eventually got the negatives back but it was a difficult process involving threats and intimidation (on her part, he was the kind of inadequate who needed to gain validation through naked pictures of his ex-girlfriend).

"So," I asked when she told me she'd got them. "Are you going to burn them now?"

"Am I Hell." She passed me the photos. "Look at me; I was only nineteen. I'll never have a figure like that again."

Carol had gone through a similar process in reverse. The sneaking and sexually exploitative conniving of her boss horrified her, but so did the sight of her middle-aged arse in nylons.

I see now what a potentially politically dodgy story it was. But the character of Carol was one I wanted to explore more. I was also in love with the setting of the old cinema. I'd worked for a while as an usherette in Glasgow's *Salon*, which claimed to be Europe's oldest cinema in continuous use (it's now a bar). I felt I could mine my experience and create an intertextual novel that wove onscreen action into the usherettes' lives. Parts of *Torchlight* are perfectly good, but as the book progressed I realised it was lacking a centre. I didn't really know what it was all about. There are worse places to be unsure of your art than an old hotel on the edge of the forest of Fontainebleau. My fellow residents were Scandinavians, visual artists who spoke English when I was around. We met each day for lunch and dinner, which we ate outside in the hotel garden and went to Paris every Friday, but otherwise set ourselves pretty strict regimes. The knowledge that the artists were in their ateliers concentrating on sculptures and paintings ensured I didn't stray too far from my desk.

I embellished Carol's world. The manager, ugly old Mr Weaver turned into a more urbane waster type, a down on his luck Brian Ferry, the sort of guy who wouldn't have the organisational skills to purchase a video camera and would rather spend the money on drink anyway. Carol gained a good-looking friend called Blythe and the cinema grew into a sparkling wreck, Gloria Swanson in *Sunset Boulevard*. But there was something missing; the central premise, the 'what if' the glue that would hold the whole range of impressions and characterisation together.

Then I got the invitation to write something else, a forty thousand-word novelette about a dead author of my choice. I knew my subject straight away, Christopher Marlowe: poet, playwright and spy.

The world of cinemas and usherettes faded and my mind shifted into the stews of sixteenth century London. I became the winner of the best post competition as books on the period started to drop through the hotel letterbox from Amazon.com. I took a seat down to the river's edge and read there until I had to admit that it was all too beautiful to concentrate and had to confine myself back in my room at the top of the house. I scattered my worktable with postcards of portraits of 16thc aristos and recounted ancient modes of punishment and torture to the Scandinavians who did me the favour of pretending to be shocked.

In her 1831 introduction to her masterpiece *Frankenstein*, written thirteen years after the book's first publication Mary Shelley writes

> And now once again I bid my hideous progeny go forth and prosper. I have an affection for it, for it was the offspring of happy days, when death and grief found no true echo in my heart. Its several pages speak of many a walk, many a drive, and many a conversation when I was not alone;

Tamburlaine Must Die is set in a different place and a different time from the one I occupied when I was writing it, but there are passages that bring back my stay in Grez-sur-Loing, the good company, the sunshine, the French food, the smell of the freshly polished woodwork in the hotel, the riverbank at the end of the garden. Grez is a village without a pub, café or restaurant so every evening around five I would go for a walk in the forest. The opening of *Tamburlaine* was conceived during these walks.

> The sun slipped lower beyond the canopy of leaves. The forest's green light deepened, tree shadows lengthened, intersecting my path like crisscrossing staves. I registered dusk's approach and walked through bars of light and dark wondering if I might employ them as a metaphor. *Nature hath no distinction twixt sun and shadow, good and evil.*

Even though I refuse to write from life, life has a way of sneaking into fiction. And what about *Torchlight*, the novel that I went to Grez to write? At present it is as neglected as that old accountancy book I found in my granddad's house. But I have plans for it. As soon as I finish the novel I'm working on I'll dig out the text because I think that at last I may have found its story. I'm heading to Canada on a residency this October and plan to have another go at it there. So perhaps that particular hideous progeny will manage to walk at last and when it does it may remind me of another country, just as *Tamburlaine Must Die* a book about another time and another place, can take me back to my months in France.

Torchlight

Prologue

Certain streets have never been respectable. Late night drunks have always stumbled on their curbs, sometimes tripping into the helpful grasp of Samaritans, who scenting a soak, right them with one steady hand and one sly, dipping pockets and smoothing lapels with the same smile. The town's litter drifts here. Empty bottles of tonic wine decorate piss-perfumed doorways and torn newspapers tumble the faces of the disappeared at the foot of alley steps. These streets are ley lines of crime crossing at murderous junctions, the lair of muggers for one hundred years. Just the spot for a night out. Where the drink is cheap and you can find company, if not in the bar rooms, then in the shadows. Mostly it's the poor who live here. But some people choose this district. They find it easiest to live where information is traded, and you only ask questions if you are willing to reveal your own game.

    Glide ciné camera smooth over tenement rooftops; halt outside lit windows and watch unseen the lives within. A girl in a stained robe crouches over the kitchen sink wrapping her wet hair in a towel. She straightens her back and sighs at the night. In the next apartment a man hunched over a table does the same calculation, over and over. His arithmetic is right but the sum comes out wrong. There's still money owed. Flit across the backcourt into a bedroom where a woman dances with her reflection, trying to drown her thoughts in the radio's blare. These are rooms where dust lingers everywhere, except the suitcase atop the wardrobe.

    One seamless swoop through a window opened a sliver, just enough to let smoke escape, and we settle on the ceiling. The proverbial fly on the wall. Our bug lens takes it all in, pans round, noting the listing corners, that give the room a Caligari feel, the red on white wallpaper, decorated with faux phoenixes, rouged and tuneless thrushes that would blister black in any fire. The camera sees the dishes resting in the sink, the baked-in spills that decorate the cooker, the Rorschach wine-splash on the rug that spells dismay. We flit over the unmade bed where the landlady's dog sighs beneath the covers. And come to rest on a figure, laid out on the couch, lead poison pale, reading a paperback thriller, the director of this show, Carol, named for Christmas, me.

> *My candle burns at both ends;*
> *It will not last the night;*
> *But oh, my foes, and oh, my friends –*
> *It gives a lovely light.*   Edna St Vincent Millais

The Picture Palace

I was intent on discovering the murderer, while at the same time trying to decide whether I was going to work that night. The two thoughts slipped side by side, until work became the killer, which seemed about right. The church on the corner chimed seven. But the murderer's knife, poised above his final victim, pinned me to the couch until a single strike of the clock announced the quarter hour and I remembered timekeeping warnings and rent owed and flung the novel to the floor.

The place had drifted into a bit of a state. The kind of condition where tidying up is like a renovation and moving starts to seem attractive. I began excavating a mound of clothing, then glanced up. Across the street a man stood silhouetted at a lit window. He looked away, quick, but a beat too slow for politeness. We'd played peepshow before, but there was no time tonight. I fastened my robe, then bundled myself in the dusty rented room curtains and dragged them shut. Yesterday's underwear sprawled half beneath the bed, my tights splayed like the undignified legs of a traffic victim. I disentangled knickers and hose, pulling them on, inside out for freshness sake, hopping perilously on one leg, then the other. Struggled with the fastenings on my bra. Shimmied into a slip, then had to root about for a safety pin to secure a strap mended only the day before. I grabbed my uniform dress from its hook, trying to smooth out the tiny hump the hours had left on it, found one shoe by the sink, its partner at the door, dabbed make-up about my face, pulled a brush though my hair, grabbed coat, bag, purse, keys, then headed out. Transformed from naked and horizontal to dressed in seven minutes and looking a mess. If I were an actress I'd have missed my cue. But I was an usherette at a cinema where most of the actresses were dead, and if I hurried it was possible no one would notice I was late.

I'd intended my job at The Picture Palace to be a brief respite. That had been two years ago. When I thought about it, which wasn't often, there were things I liked and things I didn't. Blythe was always full of plans for how life could change but then, she'd been there three years. The main thing I liked was The Palace itself. Some thrills lose their edge and others just keep kicking. The Palace was like that for me.

It wasn't a long walk from where I was staying that autumn, but it had been raining for days and somewhere along the way I had lost my umbrella. Pulling up the collar of my coat I resigned myself to wet hair and hurried along the main street dodging rain-slick brollies. It was Friday night and a frantic end of the working week feel pervaded the streets. Professional barflies would have slipped from their stools at four o'clock. They'd be safe home, in front of the television with their carryouts, leaving their seats to office workers, who even now loosened ties and tipped their chins, letting the best pint of the weekend slip down. *Ice Cold in Alex*. I hastened by the siren pubs and glowing shop windows, past the old man outside the underground, who raised his hand and smiled, not seeming to mind that I wasn't going to buy any flowers. Moon-faced George grinned at me from the window of the

French café, where he sat drinking coffee and trying the waitress's patience. A gaggle of baby goths loped past, looking too healthy for their suicide costumes, veal calf for neds. I smiled a no-change-apology to the busker, the *Big Issue* seller and the nodding head of a "hungry and homeless" man, said 'Gouranga' to the Hari Krishnas, averted my eyes from the bank where they didn't want my custom anymore. Then slipped up a darkened side street lined either side with trees.

This leg of my journey was haunted by ripper dread. I rehearsed my litany of moves. Go limp, slip from his grasp, scrape his calf, trip him, then scream and run. Or maybe I would just shit myself. The pavement here was uneven, clawed open by tree roots. I imagined the trees planning their flight, ready to scuttle along the road, shaking their branches like mad women's hair. Free at last. My heels slithered on the wet leaves that coated the cracked pavement and the trees trembled in delight. If I had my way they'd be buzz-sawed to the ground.

The Picture Palace was set slightly back from the main road, hidden until you were almost upon it. New patrons must sometimes have turned back, a yard from its entrance, convinced they had lost their way. At last I caught sight of the pink neon sign, glimmering through the leaves like a rosy halo.

Years ago brides kept a tier of their wedding cake to serve at the christening of their first child. A woman in our village kept hers in a china cabinet for twenty years. The icing had flaked from vulnerable corners, traces of mould veined its sides, but the lopsided bride and groom still held hands at its summit, tiny silver baby booties decorating their path, long after her husband had disappeared. The Picture Palace reminded me of that sometimes. Built when the trees were well manicured and the street had social standing, it was a wedding cake of a building, testament to lost dreams. Once the cinema was visible it dominated the road, and you wondered how you could ever have missed it.

The Picture Palace's frosted front was yellowed by rain, the plaster chipped in places to reveal the pink brick beneath, but The Palace was elegant in decay. Dimpled cherubs, bedecked with roses, whose tickly petals gave a squirm to their giggle hovered above a broad entrance, raising scrolled ribbons, stately as any opening night curtain. A *Sunset Boulevard* of a building, waiting for a comeback and ready for its close-up.

A miserable queue was already huddled in the rain. It was small enough to shelter beneath the building's porch, but a wooden sign staked in a weighted concrete stand, instructed them to QUEUE THIS SIDE. The instruction was supplemented by a painting of an exotically cuffed hand, pointing imperiously away from the marble steps. The 'showing tonight' sign had changed from the B movie retrospective of the week before to, "BABY MCNICHOL is *SALOME*". Mr Weaver had added the caveat, *She done him wrong!* Framing the doorway, where previously a misshapen monster crafted out of mashed potato had terrorised two sanitised sweethearts, were a pair of elegantly faded posters, mirror images of each other. A nineteen twenties silent screen siren wearing a sparkle sprigged sarong, split high to reveal dimpled legs shackled by anklets. Her chest was armoured by pearl strung breastplates and a gleaming asp, hissed Cleopatra style from the aureole of hair framing her face. It was difficult to tell if the woman was beautiful. Triangular lips and crazy kohl eyes gleamed from a china white canvas. She stood triumphal, feet splayed in ballet position one, holding the severed head of a man by his long matted hair, toasting her image on the other side of the door. The decapitated man's lolling expression, looked more real than the woman's stylised features. The image was impossible and true, repulsive and compelling.

A man at the front of the queue shuffled his feet, bringing me to my senses. I click clacked up the slippery stairs, avoiding eye contact, then pushed at the doors sending the keys rattling in their lock on the other side of the plate glass until Blythe hurried across the foyer and let me in.

*

Blythe's hair is three shades of rose gold. Her uniform, deep pink edging sweet pink, hugged her form, dipping and swooping around a wolf-whistle of a body. She takes all the clichés about Botticelli angels, wraps them up and ties a bow on them. Men buying popcorn have been known to blush when Blythe asked if they want it salty or sweet. She likes vodka twists, dry white wine, Moscow Mules, the occasional dab of speed, dancing and ugly men. There's a crease that appears just above her perfectly formed right eyebrow when she's annoyed. It makes you want to reach out and soothe it smooth. It's an urge best resisted.

"Quick, he's up in the projection booth." The crease was there, deeper than usual. Blythe stuck her head out of the door and shone her torch at the queue. A few raindrops clung to her hair. "Does he know I'm late?"

Slasher Nell the cinema cat padded up the stairs and slipped into the building. The queue edged their way towards the door encouraged by her example. Blythe smiled at them reassuringly, then slammed it shut and turned the keys in the lock.

"We'd be making arrangements to meet after the film for your leaving drink if he did." She started back up the foyer towards the refreshment counter. "You're on tickets. Where were you anyway?"

"In the middle of a good book."

Blythe raised her eyebrows, but it was an automatic response. She'd stopped being bothered.

The Palace's entrance foyer resembled an ancient court's approach to the throne of a chief. The treacherous marble stairs are a prelude to five wide carpeted steps designed to elevate mortals into the world of the movies. Gold fronds blossom into lilies on the foyer's embossed walls. A crystal chandelier glances light into a row of gilded mirrors angled to reflect a hundred chandeliers into a hundred foyers, where endless gold and glass refracts and bamboozles. The Picture Palace's wall-to-wall carpet was especially commissioned from Templeton's. Its pattern is a repeated pink double P shadowed by gold on a background of midnight blue. The letters entwine, curve facing curve, like spooning lovers.

For 70 years the Picture Palace shone. But shine takes money and there had been little of that for a while. The gold fronds had faded, the gilded mirrors grown black spotted and cloudy, the chandelier strung with cobwebs. As Blythe climbed the staircase she stepped on a slice of gaffer tape restraining a rip in the carpet. Yet the Picture Palace was still beautiful. Its dilapidation inspired a tenderness pristine pomp could never evoke.

Blythe was behind the refreshment counter straightening the bags of sweets. I leant over and put a Ruffle bar in my pocket. She looked up. "You don't even like those."

"Less calories if you don't enjoy it."

"If only."

I went into the office that doubled as a staff cloakroom as she said, "You've still to check the float."

The cramped office was always drab after the splendour of the foyer. The chipped cinema posters pinned to its nicotine walls exaggerated its decay. Airbrushed stars beamed down at the coffee stained carpet, the uneasy chairs, the ancient desk chibbed with initials. A naked 100 watt bulb flung my shadow massive against the walls. It trailed me, as I hung up my coat and started to look for a torch that could still dazzle.

Mr Weaver

There were many other things Mr Weaver could have managed. A night club that tolerated discreet dealing. A snooker hall, a casino, a spieler, a by the hour hotel. In his youth he might have been a waltzer boy, birling girls until their screams fell into gasps. Or a fly lad, punting postcards of the Eiffel Tower in hotly sealed envelopes billed, *French Photographs*. Mr Weaver might have been all these things and more. But he was perfectly suited to The Picture Palace.

It wasn't that he was a movie buff. Mr Weaver never showed any interest in the films we ran beyond slipping out of his office to watch any sex scenes from the back of the stalls. The Palace was just somehow his natural environment. I sometimes wondered if he'd ever fancied being an actor. Long years of late nights had taken their toll, giving him a tobacco tan and eyes deep creased from squinting across smoky barrooms. But you could tell he'd been handsome once. Lounging by the door, cupping a lit Bensons palmwards between his fingers he had the air of a philosophical gangster. Though with his angular gait and Brylcreamed hair he was more Peter Cushing than Humphrey Bogart.

Occasionally women would arrive towards the end of the showing and ask for Mr Weaver. They were a source of fascination to us Usherettes, who scrutinised them as we cashed up, all the better to dissect them on the way home. We decided they were dating agency fodder. The women were too consistently nervous to be professional escorts and Mr Weaver too mean to pay for anything he could get free. Blythe would sneer at them, more prescriptive than *American Vogue*, slaughtering their style from hairdo to shoe. Always concluding with, "He likes them tarty." But I was on their side. I fancied the women's wait was the first ordeal in an evening of humiliations and pitied the hopeful parade, whose expressions brightened when they saw Mr Weaver emerging tall and dark-suited into the foyer, but who never returned for a second date.

"All set girls?" Mr Weaver was wearing his second best dinner jacket. The one with the flaw in the lapel, where an enthusiastic armistice veteran had roughly stabbed a commemorative poppy. Blythe dropped from her perch on the refreshment counter, hooked open the auditorium door and stood spike in hand, ready to impale incoming tickets. "Looking lovely as usual, Blythe." He glanced at me, "Nice to see you on time Carol." then caught sight of Slasher, poised on her hind legs, front paws leaning into the popcorn basket, delicately fishing for kernels. "Oh charming. Please, don't mind me."

I wrapped my hands in a dishtowel and trying to keep out of her eye-line, grabbed Slasher and flung her into the office where she was meant to be exiled during performances. She hissed, but practice had taught me to handle the cat like an unpinned grenade and I came away unscathed.

Mr Weaver gave me a look. "Did you know she was there?"

I tried to look hurt. "No, of course not."

He didn't look convinced, but let it go with, "Nine out of ten cats may prefer popcorn, but any more of that and it's the Clyde for her. I'll do it myself with a smile on my face." It was an empty threat. Slasher was the only thing between us and the rats.

"Not a contract job then?"

"No, Blythe. Usherettes and cats I can handle myself."

Blythe muttered, "Aye, right." Under her breath but Mr Weaver either didn't hear or chose to ignore her.

"That's all I need, the environmental health down on top of me. Carol, look out for cat hairs in the popcorn tonight." There was a bang at the door. Hector, whose piano playing accompanied our silent movies, was hunched outside in his ancient leather coat, music wrapped in an off-sales carrier bag. Mr Weaver nodded. "I was just about to phone round to The Belle and see where he'd got to. Let him in, would you, Carol?"

We all knew that the idea of Hector 'getting to' anywhere other than The Belle was unlikely. Long ago he'd been in a band, on the cusp of success, an Alex Harvey meets the Blues Brothers type outfit. That was before Hector discovered the pub offered all he wanted from life. Jazzers of a certain age still remembered Orphan's Curse, perhaps all the more fondly because the band had blown it. Gigging and groupies were far behind Hector. Blythe and I were possibly the only women he talked to these days who weren't barmaids.

I opened the door and he greeted me with a weary, "All right doll?"

"All right. Yourself?"

"Aye, fine. Running a wee bit late." He gave Mr Weaver a worried nod. "All right Rab?"

"Hector, cutting it fine tonight."

Out of his natural habitat Hector assumed a ferrety aspect, glancing about as if he couldn't quite absorb the colours of the outside world after the muted tones of The Belle. "Time for a dram Rab?"

"Three minutes to showdown. You know where it is."

Hector nodded, "All right doll?" to Blythe and hurried up to the projection booth to steady his hand.

"Okay, so now we're all present and correct." Mr Weaver checked his watch against the foyer clock. It was always like that. The exact timing of the performance against a clock we all knew was synchronised not with Greenwich, but with The Belle. The queue was hovering at the doors like the freshly risen living dead from one of last season's zombie flicks. Mr Weaver looked at them and smiled. "Shall we take pity on the poor buggers or leave them standing a bit longer?" Neither of us answered. "Ach, sooner we let them in, the sooner we can all go home." He loped down the foyer, relaxed as Dean Martin at Carnegie Hall, opened the door wide and started to greet his public.

Louise Welsh – photo by Jerry Bauer

Eabhan Ní Shuileabháin

Raven

A raven barks its hard call,
Breaking through this strength of silence.

I can move again,
Put my back against rock,
Let my breath go,
Close the whites of my eyes down.

God is in the silence
And I am still frightened
Of being there all alone.

First Date

Walk slowly now, down past the Gaiety,
Take your time in this night of rain,
Keep your stomach gentle
As he asks whether you will go with him.

Keep yourself intelligent
As he kisses the inside of your hand,
Bowing his head almost reverently.
Feel his hands cupping yours,
Feel his chin and mouth warm in your grasp.

Keep yourself quiet as your heart wrenches
With the knowledge of his power,
Remember how you stumble crossing the street
This first time you walk away from him.

One for Sorrow

There is no irony left in her
to smile when he tells of those he knew
who would search the carpet pile
for fallen grains of coke,
as he himself bends to the kitchen table
to snort the non-existent powder
that may yet be clinging to its scratches.

He paces the room a hundred times,
he talks of dreams he's had
but never dared

and asserts that he is good enough
in a voice that asks for what?

The bathroom sink is stained with blood
from a nosebleed he cannot stop.

His eyes become the gravestones
of a tragedy that she has never known,
and finally there is nothing left to say,
for it's all been said, so gracefully,
so many times before.

I won't take the car, he lies to her,
I'll be back in half an hour.
Ninety minutes later, he's come to ask
if he can hold her hand, at least,
and as he finally falls asleep
he tells her that he loves her,
he loves her eyes, he loves her hair,
he loves her beyond all other cares.
And though she smells the whisky on his breath,
she still believes each word he says.

He asks her every time if she is leaving him--
She dreads the day her answer will be yes.

Featherweight
(i. m. Margaret O'Sullivan)

They say in Ancient Egypt
The test to achieve the Afterlife
Is all but impossible.
Osiris weighs the human heart
Against a feather
And only if your heart is lighter
Are you allowed admittance.

Scientists laugh at the very idea.

But I have been taught
How to make the heart so light,
For I watched you in your life.
Your heart, at the end,
Carried your soul on its back
And still weighed lighter
Than even one tiny wren's feather.

Child

I am small again,
unable to take care.
I drag my dead father,
taking him with me everywhere.

I cannot speak of him
for stumbling over
with his death-weight.

I should have buried him
these six years or more.
Instead, I daily check
the level of decay.

Immune, almost.

I have grown to like
this evidence of my devotion.
I have become twisted
and comfortable
with the carrying.

The Dark Night

This is a river I'm familiar with,
A loss that runs deep and thick
Inside my nights of wakefulness.

I am close, so close I see
The fine dark hairs on your fingers.

But you are always just not there,
Gone moments before I arrive,
The chair still warm where you sat.

I am left with messages,
Word-of-mouth assurances,
The feeling of rain in the air.

I live in a world of thunder and lightning
Knowing that you are just over there,
Counting, always counting the distance between us
Unable to find you right here.

The Friendship Monument

P F Brownsey

First there's the stab of alarm and then Muir realises why he felt it: he's been so absorbed in leaflets in Huntly tourist office that he's forgotten Andrew Garvie.

But Andrew Garvie is just standing at rest, hands in the pockets of his zip-up jacket, not looking at things, not filling in time. So contained. The grey in the black hair somehow isn't connected with the ageing process, the moustache not something he's chosen to wear, the glasses are a permanent emblem of intelligence, not a remedy for weakening eyesight.

Still, there's no need for Muir to feel like a small boy who's stopped out to play beyond the parental curfew. He's Andrew Garvie's boss, in effect. As college dean he'd have a big say if Garvie applied for promotion. Or there was ever any sort or complaint against him.

"My wife always said I lost myself in whatever was in front of my eyes." It's the affable voice with which Muir hands round the dean's whisky, though what he actually hands Garvie is a leaflet. He doesn't add that his capacity for losing himself in things had seemed to irritate Sheila, like so much else. "The Friendship Monument. Someone put up a monument to friendship in his front garden. I could do with some friends." He laughs quickly. "A hulking great thing with all his friends' names on it. We could take a look. Durrie isn't far."

"Could do worse," says Andrew Garvie obligingly.

"Thank you." As they drive off Muir finds himself applying Andrew Garvie's remark to Andrew himself as a holiday companion. They don't squabble. But then, two men in their forties wouldn't squabble. It's children who squabble, like Gavin and Emma.

He'd been surprised after the divorce at the number of people who'd taken it on themselves to tell him he needed a holiday: wasn't advice the prerogative of friends? What's more, they said he mustn't go on holiday by himself or he'd brood. All this was data to be fed into the decision-making process. No doubt brooding was something people did and would be unhealthy. After the separation Muir had simply worked harder than ever, and that's really when he'd made sure of the deanship. Of course, it was taking a risk, going on holiday with someone you're in authority over. But it's possible to be mature and not let personal feelings get in the way of work's demands, management structure, procedures.

Sheila once said: "Muir Maxwell, you've got procedures for being a husband."

It had been taking a risk in another way, too. Garvie never alluded being homosexual. He had murmured in the Huntly news-agent's, "*Gay Times* on sale in deepest Aberdeenshire!" but the way he said it, he might have been referring to a magazine about coin collecting, and he'd made no move to touch it. And although in their hotel room at night Garvie undressed completely and got into bed nude, he did it with such perfect chasteness, so much just as a matter of course, that Muir, in his twin bed, had an obscure feeling that he was doing Garvie an injustice by wearing his pyjamas.

Muir would say he is enjoying his holiday as they round a corner and the full descending sweep of the huge country opens up to receive them. Having taught English literature before moving into administration, Muir can docket what he sees. Fields and crops and the rich earth signify that life is fundamentally benign, the unclouded sunshine discloses values clear and pure, distant farms are outposts of a better life, the little fold of cottages which is their destination beckons with a promise of peace. By contrast, towns mean misery, alienation, degradation, vice …

"There it is!"

"Sorry." Inadvertently Muir has driven past it. But, my, yes, it is impressive, height and mass accentuated by the road's dipping below a walled bank just here.

It's meant to be approached from the road below. The hedge is cut away in framing curves to present the Friendship Monument like a shrine, like a war memorial. But as Muir ascends the narrow steps nothing could be further from the serene lines of cross or cenotaph. It must be 20 feet high, it has no formal shape, it thrusts upwards like a giant canine tooth tearing into things, it threatens to topple on you, crush you. Though presumably the authorities have established that it's safe. The surrounding hedge is trimmed very neatly and the joins between the flagstones underfoot have been carefully weeded. The hedge screens all but the double-dormered roof of the dwelling-house at the rear, of which this was once the front garden.

Muir, from his leaflet, says encouragingly: "He was called Lionel Christie. He was wounded in the last war. His brother was the local minister and brought him here to recuperate. Apparently he only lived on for four or five years. All alone in the cottage behind."

In places the raw stone has been smoothed into panels. One bears the word "Friendship" in large letters of gold, and below, smaller: "Enduring as breath, quick to death." Other panels present a long alphabetical list of gilded names. It says at the head, "In them friendship died."

Muir remarks, "He seems to have listed only dead friends."

"Maybe he thought the living ones wouldn't last the course."

Keith Adamson, Stuart Ainsworth, Roger Bradley … What a treasure is in these names! The invisible fibres connecting the dead man to each and every one of these unknown people draw substance and density into him.

Muir begins a mental recitation of every name on the list.

Garvie is staring at the monument like someone trying to work out how a conjuror's trick is done. "A couple of hundred names. People on a Christmas card list, maybe, but you couldn't have that many friends."

"Oh, but think of all the people we work with. Once you add up people you know … "

"Friends aren't just people you know."

At the management training course Personnel had said that in dealing with disputes one should first try to find something that both parties were happy with. Muir says, "Perhaps it was people he knew in the army. That could explain why he's listed only dead people. Perhaps they were in some big slaughter like the Normandy landings. Listing them as friends is an accolade: they're not just fellow-soldiers, they're friends. They could hardly be people he knew here, he was so isolated, and unable to get about with his wound."

Euan Campbell, Fergus Campbell, Murray Downie, Patrick Duffus ...

Muir says, "And if they're his fellow-soldiers, that could explain why there are no women's names."

Garvie points to names that Muir's recitation hasn't yet reached: Shirley Mitchinson, Christine Stevenson, Joan Tebbutt, Carole Young. That last one is at the bottom, above the closing inscription: "All dead, living and dead."

Muir snaps, "Well, then, perhaps it's something else."

He'd *never* shown anger to Sheila. Sweet-looking, that was what she used to say he was. Though she made it sound as if it were a contemptible thing to look. Unless she meant that he was only sweet-*looking*, not genuinely sweet-natured. Still, as dean you couldn't afford to be sweet to all and sundry, you had tough decisions to make.

Muir says cheerfully, "Still, what an obsession, to put all your time and energy and money into this. I mean, I value my friends as much as the next man, but ..." He tries to think of names he could put up unhesitatingly if he were to erect a similar monument.

Garvie is looking on tip-toe over the rear hedge. "There's a visitor centre in the house." Obligingly Muir abandons his incomplete rosary.

"Christ, they milk the monument for all it's worth," Garvie says inside. You can buy car stickers, mugs, pennants, kitchen aprons, badges, all printed with slogans like *Durrie – the Friendship Village* and *Friendship – Made in Durrie*. A dish towel exhibits a recipe for friendship: six good turns, one shared outlook, generous pinch of loyalty, long slow cooking. You can buy a friendship-pledging certificate, ornately printed, with places for two people to sign. There are books with appropriate titles: *Our Mutual Friend*, *Testament of Friendship*, *Iris and the Friends*, *Letters to a Friend*, Francis Gay's *Friendship Book*. There are videos of *Friends* from television, which Gavin and Emma always want to watch, though the jokes can be a bit ... There are oat-cakes and tablet and heather perfumes, gift-wrapped and inscribed *From a friend to a friend from Durrie, the Friendship Village*.

"Needs a comma after the second 'friend'," says Andrew Garvie. "Otherwise you're saying your friend comes from Durrie."

"Still, everything has to sell itself these days," says Muir, thinking of the increased budgets for artwork and jazzy layouts that he has to approve for the college's publicity.

But there are also exhibits of genuine interest. Display cases contain memorabilia of Lionel Christie: letters, photographs, medals he won in the war, designs for the monument. In the photos he's usually on his own. A 1940s film star's smooth good looks and a manly pipe radiate the courage and confidence that won the war.

On the wall are framed newspaper cuttings, surprisingly unyellowed. *Ex-soldier Raises Monument to Friends* quotes Christie: "If the value of a life lies in the friends one makes, the value of my life will be evident to all."

Another reports an inauguration ceremony. The minister-brother had pronounced a blessing. He and his wife and Lionel Christie had been the only people present. A photo shows them smiling half a century ago beneath the monolith; the hedge hasn't yet grown. The three had sung the children's hymn, 'There's a friend for little children above the bright blue sky.' Christie is quoted: "I chose it because to believe in friendship one needs to be as a little child."

Under a sub-heading *Absent Friends* the newspaper continues: "Although the monument commemorates 162 friends, none of them was invited to the ceremony. Captain Christie explained, 'They would be no more my friends by their presence than in their absence'."

"Obviously an eccentric," says Muir, without judgement, for a dean has to handle all types, as they sit down at a table with their tea. "Still," he says, "we all need friends."

At another table two noisy children, a boy and a girl, are being shushed by their mother, the father conspicuously leaving this to her. But perhaps he isn't their father, perhaps he's their mother's 'boyfriend', perhaps this scene is the duplicate of others involving Gavin and Emma ...

"It must be tough." Garvie has read his mind, pressed his arm.

Muir puts aside the comfort. If Sheila knew he went on holiday with a homosexual who presses his arm would she try to use it to restrict access still further?

"You see, Andrew, in the country people have a different sort of connection than in towns and cities. Deeper. You may not see as much of other people, you're isolated, but they matter more to you so it's natural to refer to them as friends. The names could be people in cottages and farms around him. And that would explain so few women: country respectability. It could cause comment, putting a woman's name on the monument."

But Andrew Garvie is on his feet, is saying, "I'll be right back," is out the door. Its shutting rebukes Muir for ignoring his gesture of comfort.

Muir flinches again when Garvie returns and says, "I thought so."

Garvie announces, "It's not a monument to friendship, it's a monument to the lack of friendship. It's saying friendship is a sham."

"Shh." Muir looks apologetically at the mother.

"'All dead, living and dead.' They're dead as friends, is what he means, even if they're still alive."

"I can't allow that, Andrew." The dean has been forced to assert himself, for the proposal would absolutely empty the budget. "No-one would put up a monument to not having friends."

"And as for 'Enduring as breath' – "

"Breath lasts as long as life itself, Andrew."

"A breath lasts three seconds."

"Your tea's getting cold."

"What the – ?" Garvie notices that his tea-cup has been replaced by, his tea decanted into, a mug that reads *I've been to Durrie and I'll be your friend*.

"Little present." Muir hopes he is twinkling at Garvie.

"And friendship is 'Quick to death'."

"'Quick' can mean 'alive', Andrew."

"Look, Christie is right!" The ferocity carries over into: "Thanks for the mug. I appreciate it."

Andrew Garvie continues like someone wheeling on decisive evidence about the Friendship Monument. "There was this guy, Tam Gallagher. We were at school together, bought motorbikes, spent Saturdays tinkering with them together. Did all the teenager things together: slipping into pubs, getting drunk the first time, going to discos."

Muir listens to important information about himself that has always been withheld.

"When he was, what, twenty-four, he bought a flat and he phones up and asks me to go round to help him lay a carpet. I couldn't go at once, I was accompanying my Mum to the hospital, they'd found a lump in a breast though she didn't want it known. Tam Gallagher hears my hesitation and says, 'I'm not being any trouble, am I?' And I said, 'Well, just now, yes.' And he says, sarcastic, 'Thanks a lot.' And *that was that!* He rang off, gave me no chance to explain, I never heard from him again. I tried contacting him, got nowhere. So what was that so-called friendship between us all those years? Nothing. No connection, no bond. We occupied adjacent space, that's all.

"And when I first came out, went on the gay scene …"

Muir can't ask whether Andrew Garvie had made some sort of pass at the Gallagher person.

"… I was befriended," Andrew Garvie is saying, "by this guy, Donald Scobie. He was slightly fey, slightly camp. Awfully attentive, though not in a romantic way. Did you ever have that experience of going to a new school and the teacher appoints an existing pupil to be friends with the new boy, show him around, etcetera? That was Donald, he loved the role. Explained everything, who everyone was, where to go or not go, people to be wary of. Stuff I was ignorant of, like whether you could swallow semen."

The children! Muir nods warningly towards them.

"Even introduced me to people I said I fancied. Seemed to have no lovelife of his own. He was always on the phone. Sometimes just to say, 'It's raining here. Is it raining where you are?' He gave tremendously expensive presents at Christmas. I was embarrassed but when I tried to talk about a limit he just said, 'You give according to how much you value a person. I value your friendship more than you value mine, that's all there is to it, nothing to worry about.' And he meant it, he wasn't being sarky. I liked him more and more, I began to think I had a real friend in Donald."

"When my mother died he was wonderful, helping to sort her things, tremendously sensitive. I was getting rid of most of her furniture and when Donald asked me what was I doing with her fridge I said, 'Maybe I'll get twenty quid for it'. He turned away and took the huff and wouldn't speak. When I realised he'd been asking for himself I apologised and said of course I'd be happy to give it to him. But he still wouldn't speak. He got up and left. And that was that. Never spoke to me again. How could that have been friendship, to be destroyed by a wee misunderstanding over a second-hand fridge? No, no, that isn't a monument to friendship, Christie *knew*."

"Oh, but – "

Muir realises he was about to continue, "… that was a homosexual." Homosexuals were well known to be emotional. He says instead, like someone speaking from the midst of a network of ripe enduring uncomplicated friendships, "You've had some unfortunate experiences." Kindly, he offers Andrew Garvie a similar incident from his own life.

He says, "When Sheila was a student she was friendly with a girl from a very respectable background."

Muir tastes again the feeling of being absolutely unworried that Helen Merchiston could give him just by the way she said, "Hello, Muir." Of course, there was never any question of anything romantic between them, for he'd attached himself to Sheila when they both helped run the church youth club and had never looked beyond her for a social life.

"Helen, this girl, was very slim and refined in manner, though absolutely uninhibited in what she would talk about. Sex. Very coarsely. She had an unfortunate time. She became a single mother in the days when that caused more problems than it does today. It made no difference to Sheila, Sheila was always ready to help her out, always baby-sitting for her. Though that only enabled her to get involved with other unsuitable men, until she became pregnant again. I didn't know about it at the time, of course. Sheila put up the money for her to have an abortion, which wasn't so easy in those days. Afterwards Sheila never heard from her again. And she made absolutely no attempt to repay Sheila the money. Oh no, it would be too vulgar for a young lady from Kelvinside to repay money that could be ill-spared by us, we were saving for our wedding!"

"Still, people move on," he says, having heard the phrase and added it to his wisdom.

"Exactly. Friendship dies. People fucking *move on*."

"Would you mind your language, please? There are children here." The mother. The boyfriend looks away. Muir suddenly understands that the boyfriend doesn't want to back up the mother, in case she takes it as a signal of commitment: I'm your defender.

That's one in the eye for Sheila. Imperceptive about people and feelings, was he? He says cheerfully, "Sheila thought the explanation was that she was too much associated in Helen's mind with a very painful time."

"If that killed it, it was never friendship. People think they're friends and they're just passing shadows to each other. Isolated and solitary and hard. Like that monument."

"You're wrong, Andrew, you're wrong," Muir cries, and the stares of the woman and the boyfriend and the children, directed at him now, tell him how loudly he cried it.

He laughs affably. "And since you're in the maths department we'll overlook the mixed metaphor."

Here's another one in the eye for anyone who says he's no good on things like feelings and relationships. Neither of Garvie's stories was about someone ending a friendship because he's a homosexual. But that must have happened time and again. Why didn't he mention one of those cases? Because those rejections would have been the most hurtful of all! Yes, you can see why he is set on rubbishing the Friendship Monument.

Which he does again as they leave. While Muir is unlocking the car Andrew Garvie stands at the foot of the steps, staring up at the monument. The angle heightens its huge rearing glittery-grey menace against the now-overcast sky. He's holding Muir's mug by the handle, carefully, as though it were full: *I've been to Durrie and I'll be your friend*. He says, "Well, the worth of his life is evident enough. He told the truth."

"It's like something from the prehistoric stone circle at Easter Aquho-however-you-pronounce-it." Muir cheerily recalls their visit of the day before.

"Quite a phallic symbol for Aberdeenshire," says Andrew Garvie.

It is with delight, as he drives them up from Durrie, that Muir thinks of the complete answer to Garvie's negative response to the Friendship Monument, this insistent brooding on broken friendships which is perhaps a little immature for a senior position. "You know, Andrew, you're wrong. You say friendship doesn't exist. Isn't the real refutation this, that *you* were so ready to be friends with these people, that *you* would have continued to be a good, loyal friend? I'm sure you would have done!"

That is what he thinks of saying, accompanied by the dean's encouraging twinkle. It's the dean's job to encourage. But the leaden sky is too pressing, the immense folds of hills and fields seem poised to overwhelm the little cluster of houses they're leaving behind, you could fancy a malign power in the land that the network of hedges and roads is too flimsy to contain. Ah yes, the literary tradition of the country as a place of blighting forces, brutality, fear. Thomas Hardy. However, when they retire for the night to their twin beds at the hotel in Banchory Muir makes amends to Garvie for this silence. He sets aside his pyjamas as though he couldn't understand what they were doing in his bed. He undresses completely, gets into bed nude. Garvie, quite properly, appears not to notice. It can make absolutely no difference, if and when he has to comment on Andrew Garvie's application for promotion.

Rody Gorman

Melting Point
(après Mark Lynas)

Back in a corrie in the highland area
of the Cordillera Blanca, Peru,
having passed over a shoal of talus
without a handhold or karabiner

and runoff to a terminal moraine,
at a loss for words, our craggy ghillie
Hector MacDonald lets go the belay anchor
and looks up at a cairn on the horizon

in the rarefied air around Huascaran,
Huayhuash, Cashan, Jacabamba,
the séracs, the couloirs, the bergschrunds,

the soft névé, the glacier deliquescing under Artesonraju,
tongue 500 metres further away than before
and cries out: *Ice field, is it? Ice fank, more like.*

In Memoriam Leslie Quirk (1914 – 2004)

Still active, he spoke out from the bed
in his chosen language
to us, familiar and alien at once,
not officially dead
but, then, officially never in existence.

He just went on and on
and gave us *Ellan Vannin Veg Veen,*
A Short History of the Manx Language
and a brand-new edition
of *Bible Chasherick yn Lught Thie.*

On the way back from the home
(it was time for evensong)
in Peel, we passed by the strand
and watched the same *John Deere*
which was there the night before

and which, according to the tide,
goes out and cleans the sand.
Tomorrow evening
when the tide's right he'll be back there
and he'll do it all over again.

Moose

After the gym and McDonald's in Sydney,
Jim is telling us about Hector MacDonald
from between Big Pond and Ben Eoin,
last native speaker of the *tok ples* there:
One strong bodach!
He was known as Moose.

On the Guinness, Hector was in a car-crash
and lost his limbs in it, says Jim,
but it never stopped him –
he kept on cracking away
all the same every minute
right up until the end.

Back home that night, herself who's gone
and done us cold-pressed ox-tongue
à la Mrs. Beeton, with cashaw squash and pecan,
succotash and char, after grace
has been said, asks: *Everything okay? Fine,
Mrs Campbell,* I reply. *Everything's fine.*

Déjà Vécu

I don't think I can take it any more.
We watch the evening news from Network Three.
She says: *I've seen and heard it all before.*

I try Palak Paneer from Bangalore.
Had it she says *Prefer my Rosie Lee.*
I don't think I can take it any more.

She says that all along she knew the score
in tonight's local derby from Dundee.
She says: *I've seen and heard it all before.*

She'd never met Su Wong from Singapore
and when she did she said: *Long time no see!*
I don't think I can take it any more.

She throws *The Independent* on the floor.
The tray her tea's on falls off the settee.
She says: *I've seen and heard it all before.*

I'm out of here. I'm heading for the door.
I've had enough. I've somewhere else to be.
I don't think I can take it any more.
She says: I've seen and heard it all before.

Mr MacMillan and Mr MacLeod

Nineteen sixty three?
I don't mind where I was
when the story about Kennedy
was breaking on the wireless

but I do mind
Mr. MacMillan and Mr. MacLeod,
out late of an evening with Daddy
and the Lochmor passing on the Sound

and the wind
and then that big old
pink sun over the island
and next minute it was all gone.

Slàinte!

You know the way
    the Gaels have a name
        for drink

and whisky
    is the oldest and best-known word
        of theirs in English?

Well, the great academic, Alexander MacDonald,
    on the shot and batter the other day
        in the bodach's house

(he'd cleared all the outhouses
    of their gear,
        including stuff belonging to his grandfather

and sold up
    all the sheep
        for the central slaughterhouse in Inverness),

belting out a whole corpus of songs:
    Murt na Ceapaich and *Murt Ghlinne Comhann,*
        Cumha Alasdair Dhuinn,

'S e mo bheachd ort, a bhàis,
    Hì ri o ho, luidh leo iù bho,
        Hì rim ho ro,

had had so much
    he took it away
        and emptied the full Isle of Jura down the sink.

November Nineteen Sixty Two

Our father, who's never had a motor-car before,
is not awfully sure where we're going to.
Mother directs him through Tullamore,
Birr, home. It's November Nineteen Sixty Two.

The lock opens before us and we drive
over the top and backfire like a cannon.
We get a shock – *Man alive!*
It's Bonaparte himself crossing the Shannon!

Mother reads us *Three Little Pigs* after bath,
done all together. They listen to the President
on the wireless. Kathleen looks like Sylvia Plath.
Kennedy? says Grandfather – *Borrisokane, is it?*

The two men are up in a flash and away
while all the others are still in bed.
Not a sound between them. Another day.
The bonhams are waiting to be fed.

Ashaig

In Ashaig (Scottish Gaelic *aiseag*
return, restoration, ferry,
deliverance, rendering)

where St. Mulree crossed over in a Boyne *pirogue*
filled with Torridonian sandstone,
Lewisian gneiss and limestone, beside the oratory,

being forced under by the shore
and all that bone,
they've resurfaced the runway

to transport souls every day
in vivireceptacles before they've all gone
off to the other side.

Teangue, Isle of Skye

Near where the *Claymore* went down,
Tyboran Fisk in the carrageen and wrack,
dead calm, a Manx shearwater on a rock.

an empty can, a sheen,
a line of black
from here to the end
of the shore, a brogue
barely moving on the sound.

Reviews

Morgan/Grahamilia

Aspects of Form and Genre in the Poetry of Edwin Morgan, Rodney Stenning Edgecombe, Scholars Press, £29.99; *English Texts and Studies* 43, Ralph Pite and Hester Jones, *W S Graham: Speaking Towards You*, Liverpool, £20.00); *Representing Scotland in Literature, Popular Culture and Iconography: The Maskes of the Modern Nationanlism* Alan Riach, Palgrave Macmillan, £60.

The reputations of Edwin Morgan and W S Graham could not be more different. Despite initial bureaucratic argy-bargy about stipend, remit and function, Morgan was announced first 'Makar of Scotland', and produced two poems for the Scottish Parliament. His work is a staple of the educational system in Scotland. The Creative Writing school in Glasgow is named after him, and, although Carcanet published his *Collected Poems* in 1990, any observer of Scottish literature will no doubt own works published by Mariscat since then; *Demon, Love and a Life* and *Tales from Baron Munchausen*, as well as Carcanet's supplemental volume *Cathures*.

The first passably complete edition of W S Graham, who died in 1986, was published by Faber & Faber in 2004. Although it restores many of the posthumous collections – *Aimed at Nobody* and *Uncollected Poems*, much of Graham's prose and prose-poetry is still unavailable. Graham is famous for not being famous; a talisman for avant-garde anthologists. In Iain Sinclair's anthology *Conductors of Chaos* (1996), Graham, along with David Gascoyne, J F Hendry, David Jones and Nicholas Moore, is presented as a forebear of the 'alternative' tradition in poetry.

Such a polarisation is unsatisfactory. Morgan himself has written sympathetically on Graham, yet was curiously omitted from Keith Tuma's anthology of 20th century poetry. And in critical appreciation, Graham now far outstrips Morgan, as evidenced by the first two volumes under consideration.

One salient fact: Graham is dead and Morgan is alive. Any critic pronouncing on the work of a living author is a hostage to fortune. In 2002, the editors of *Poetry Review* commissioned a long piece from me on Morgan's poetry (their decision to showcase Morgan reveals much about his centrality to contemporary debates on poetry). Reading Morgan again, I thought about his chameleon-like adoption of masks and personae, and toyed with relating this to strategies for dealing with homosexual identity. The argument, had I committed it to print, would have been that Morgan assumes and evades, that he, as a product of a repressive *milieu*, found it difficult to write, 'out' poetry. Within a year, Morgan published the tender, beautifully unambiguous autobiographical collection "Love and a Life". He's still ahead of his critics, and I hope he eludes us all for many more years. With Graham, the critic is dealing with an intact oeuvre, a discrete unit: though that too has odd implications for his work.

The criticism there is of Morgan is dated. Apart from the volume under consideration, the only other monograph is Colin Nicholson's *Edwin Morgan: The Invention of Modernity*, Manchester UP, and the subject of a justly withering review in the *TLS* by James W Wood. There are collections with important material – including Robert Crawford and Hamish Whyte's *About Edwin Morgan*. 1990 and *Chapman* 64 (1991), as well as the Poetry Library's *Unknown is Best*, for Morgan's 80th birthday, and numerous individual papers in academic journals. So any new monograph is a welcome and brave entry into the field.

Edgecombe's *Aspects of Form and Genre in the Poetry of Edwin Morgan* deals with five major areas: vision poems, the 'travel' poems *The Cape of Good Hope* and *The New Divan*, the grotesque, the elegiac and the dramatic monologues. In writing about a poet as compendious and protean as Morgan, there must be a necessary limitation for the critic: it seems suspect to omit discussion of translations, concrete poetry, sound poetry, sonnets, catalogues (especially the *Alphabet of Goddesses*) and newspoems.

The most interesting chapter deals with *The New Divan*, a poem Morgan insists is central to his career and yet attracts very little detailed consideration. Edgecombe opens his discussion with a pertinent, Morgan-esque, image: *"Rather like the Windows"* computer programme, *The New Divan* opens several files at once, and keeps them open while it shifts them round the screen". Sadly, Edgecombe does not pursue the analogy in his interpretation. Despite realising the aleatory, conversational and deliberately disjunctive nature of the poem, the critic attempts to impose a narrative over the shifting textures of the collection. Individual readings of individual poems are handled well, but Edgecombe might have considered ulterior meanings of 'divan' – not just "a collection of poems" or "an Eastern couch" but "a council of state: a court of justice". It seems typical of Morgan to elide luxuriance with determination, and repose with social conscience.

Edgecombe discusses works given less attention: *The Vision of Cathkin Braes*, *The Whittrick* and the Instamatic poems. The section on dramatic monologues would benefit from reference to poems like 'Byron at Sixty-Five', 'Cinquevalli', 'Instructions to an Actor' or the poems in *Star Gate*. Perhaps the most detrimental flaw is an academic pretentiousness. Why should a poet as accommodating and communicative as Morgan be slathered with words like "hodoiporika", "transvaluation" and "aposematic"? But were *Chapman* to update their Morgan festschrift of the 90s, Edgecombe would be an interesting and valued contributor.

Criticism of W S Graham is more subtle and self-confident. Salt, Cambridge-based publishers, produced a wonderful monograph, *Where the People Are: Language and Community in the Poetry of W S Graham*, by Matthew Francis and Tony Lopez, *The Poetry of W S Graham* (1989) is an erudite and essential starting-point. Edited by Ralph Pite and Hester Jones, *W S Graham: Speaking Towards You* is a wide-ranging study, which opens new vistas of interpretation. Matthew Francis provides a fine essay, 'Syntax Gram and the Magic Typewriter: W S Graham's Automatic Writing', providing a radical, compelling reading of a body of work in need of wider circulation. The editors have excellent essays on Graham and the St Ives abstract art community (by Pite) and numinous mysticism (by Jones). Special mention to Peter Robinson's essay on dependence, Ian Sansom's look at the dual pull of Scotland and the Black Mountain, and Adam Piette's elegant analysis of line-breaks.

It's good to see writers wrestling with how to classify Graham, *vide* range of authors he is compared with: Larkin, Thomas, Rimbaud, Mallarmé, Eliot, Trakl ... The linguistic arguments that underpin his work are expertly unpicked; Graham knew, almost somatically, the ideas of Heidegger and Derrida. The strangest aspect of Graham is the preternatural sense that the poems were written with the foreknowledge that they would be read after his death – like Lowry, who used glazes that would only effect the painting long after he could see them, Graham constructed a poetics founded in the absence of the author, the white of the page, and the almost miraculous capacity to transmit these across time. If Morgan is ahead of the critics in life, Graham is ahead of the reader in death. He almost beckons into silence.

Two poets of intelligence, awful awareness, and sly manner: is it any wonder that Scotland finds it difficult to encompass its authors? Is there a way out of the current slough of '100 Best', 'Nation's Greatest' and silly surveys of dubious integrity? The fact that there are monographs on these two poets is heartening: rather than yet another Jabberwocky quest after the quintessence of 'Scottishness', sharp-eyed readings of individual authors will doubtless clarify what we mean by poetry, Scotland and 'Scottish Poetry'.

Alan Riach is the best guide to the future we have. In *Representing Scotland*, he does exactly what the "re" in the title implies: this is a book re-thinking rather than a reference book. There are sensitive and revealing readings of 'key' Scottish texts – Scott, Stevenson and Buchan – alongside more guerrilla expeditions. Riach has a wonderful aside on a poem by Morgan far more daring than Edgecombe's essays into the hinterlands of Morganistan. He writes about MacDiarmid with a mature sense of the importance, and problems, of such a torrential author. But it is when he strays from the path of conventional academia that Riach comes into his own.

James Bond. Mendelssohn. Lobey Dosser. Batman. Amos Tutuola. Shakespeare. Riach is magpie-sharp at snatching the coincidences of a broader Scottish culture into an argument about how we might become ourselves. This is not a book propounding destinations, but a manual of possible routes. He is especially good on graphic novels, giving them the attention they deserve.

Riach is an exemplar of close reading: take the argument he can find in on variation between the Quarto and the Folio of Shakespeare's *King Lear*. A single letter ('s') can be unravelled into multitudes. I have rarely come across a work that matches its diligence with its exuberance. Some academics try to bridge the divide, and often sink in a swamp of bad puns; Riach has an integrity of vision and rigour of reading that single him out from the lumpen professoriat.

The theory of masks Riach offers is classically Scottish: we assume and dispose of identities faster than Picasso on acid. But some of those masks – British intelligence agent, colonial oppressor, maudlin drunk and angry reformer – are useful for a while. But we need to investigate our plurality with more self-awareness, if we are to avoid self-stereotypes, or having a stereotype put upon us. There is surely room in Scotland for Morgan and W S Graham, Iain Hamilton Finlay and Tim Stead, The League of Extraordinary Gentlemen and Oor Wullie. Riach points a way beyond our national bipolarity; and those who do not follow will be forgotten.

The Cultural Commission

540 pages. £500,000. But only a further 100 copies of the "Commision" report (sic) will be printed. So if you want the low-down, over to you to download from their website!

At £925.92 per page, the report from the Cultural Commission is a major event for the arts in Scotland. It is, perhaps, a tear, a rip into the mundanity of cultural debate, which allows real thinking to occur. The report is not cut and dried – will require several parliamentary bills before implemation – and it is urgent for Scotland's writers to understand and evaluate the proposals put forward by James Boyle and the Commission.

The only reference to literary magazines in the report comes in a section about Gaelic publishing. Despite its championing of language and writing, literature is given scant attention, and often-erroneous claims are made about the current state of literature. The Book Festival is, we learn, "vulnerable", since not enough money is spent on attracting the best managers. Given Catherine Lockerbie's sterling efforts, the best one can say is that the Commission did not have time to see Charlotte Square last summer, read the programme, attend enough events *(other than those wine-laced!)* or observe Ms Lockerbie's enthusiasm, diligence or kindness.

There are four major aspects *which should be the subject of hard thinking*. The first is that there will be no more Arts Council: the new Culture Scotland will rise, phoenix-style, from its ashes. The aesthetic and financial judgements will be made separately (and one wonders how one body can advise the national companies, individual entrepreneurs and the actual producers of the raw material: hands up! Who among you *also* has a business plan?). Come 2008, we will all be able to judge the new hoops we may have to jump through for funding – we've only just got the hang of filling in the old forms! The most important difference may be none at all. Bureaucratic change means nothing until we know to whom applications might be made.

Culture Scotland will have two more staff

than the bodies it will assimilate; there will, however, be redundancies. Whether artists are to deal with New Brooms, Trusted Colleagues or Usual Suspects is unknown.

Then we have that old chestnut, taxation. The report recommends that the Culture Minister persuades Gordon Brown that 'creative' types get £30,000 income not subject to income tax. If Brown goes mad and approves this, it might allow journalists (ie those who hack into their literary lives to make ends meet), to claim exemption on the basis of a few poems; it might encourage writers to move to Scotland as a loop-hole, while contributing nothing else. What about the plumbers, electricians, carpenters and joiners whose work is no less creative. When even the Irish, whose system the Scottish model is based on, are reconsidering, why are we entertaining such a problematic *state*?

Then there is the proposal for the "Academy", real title still pending. That the best Scottish writers should be given recognition seems indisputable. But who elects these grandees? Who should even be in the running? I bet J K Rowling and Quentin Jardine, Alasdair Gray and A L Kennedy would be the first to nominate others as more deserving!

Finally, the idea for a "Scottish Centre for the Book". Combining the work of the Publisher's Association, the Book Festival, City of Literature and, maybe, Scottish PEN: why should these be clumped together? The *status quo* works; Book Trust and Poetry Library provide attractive spaces. Who will govern the "Book Centre"? Who negotiates between the bodies housed in this building? What about the Book Festival's sensible *coup* in moving to Charlotte Square? Who has asked the bodies in question? *Non fiat Boyle-o.*

The Commission is an opportunity, not an imposition. Writers should decide what they believe is the solution to the disparity in funding, the status of the respective bodies, the role of agencies and the fiscal problems. Most of us have already spoken, and been ignored, but if we do not speak, again, we will be told what to do.   *S B Kelly*

Give in to the Spell
Chapman Authors 107

Richard Burns, Father of the Cambridge Poetry Festival, releases astounding, often-overlooked work in *For the Living: Selected Writings 1, Longer Poems 1965-2000* (Salt, £10.95). Starting with 'The Easter Rising 1967', written in Thebes after the *coup d'état* in April, 1967, Burns destroys and humanises notions of political right and wrong: "They are all innocent/But I am sick of innocence/ Lord I have lost my delight …/ Oh God I am sick of the conversation/ of all my friends."

It takes effort not to read 'conversion' instead of 'conversation', 'criminals' for 'innocent'. The God of this book grows heavier and heavier. In 1968 'Easter Rising' was published in *London Magazine* under the "pseudonym Agnostos Nomolos" ('Solomon', backwards), believed a "young Greek poet" that had "smuggled [the poem] out of Greece". Burns presented himself "as the poem's translator. Many London literati fell for this … though they may well have had their suspicions". Burns easily shape-shifts into other people, multiple countries, crumbling masses of land and skin.

Burns asks how rituals first sculpted us and into which strange forms they plan to make us. It is a question of politics, but it isn't political; it is life "for the living". In 'Avebury', images shift in an *Exorcist*-like panoramic twist: "your eyelids/ jumping like fish/ veil nothing here/ you are the very/ shadow you discarded/ all is eyes". After wading through the prose poems, whether he's with an old man in Greece staring at the man who asked, "What's the use of poets in a mean-spirited age?" or reconstructing Breton legends of crystal cities, you feel as if you've nibbled a magic fungus and gone back to mystic-history class for sceptical adults, with Burns as storyteller and Trickster, at the head of the class. His unique type of internationally minded, careful, surreal prodding may be just what we need to find out, as he asks in 'Easter Rising', "Are we/ Or they/ Imprisoned?" It is well worth giving in to his spell.

Donald Smith also pokes with a theatrical, sharpened prod and refuses to let up in *A Long Stride Shortens the Road: Poems of Scotland* (Luath, £8.99). Funny, lush, and immense, it turns Scotland tropical, makes its stories fecund so that we watch them sprout. In 'Citadels', we go "… to the Castle Rock/ the Crown of Scotland where eye bejewelled bedazzled/ gazes on the pilgrim's prize/ relics of our nationhood." How quickly prizes become relics. Smith further asks where the head has gone that once held up that "crown", asks what "the minister's wife" is thinking:

> her look the courage
> of the gently worn down
> a portrait in the drawing room
> she sits at night
> embroidering the fall.

Fields of excess and perfectly framed pictures are used to demonstrate lack and hidden, silent movements. The "fall" carries with it a bitter season and a broken Eden forgotten, repeated. "Unfinished absence", he writes in 'Tusitala', for RLS, "to be haunting/ the same moment". No one is able to shake their ghosts, but that's OK, we can play with them if we learn their language. Gaelic birdsongs flutter around a hike, James VI of Scotland (James I of England) has a run-in with a skull in the quirky historical play, 'Preface to Cradle King', and in 'Tusitala', Smith incants, "Tusitala/ your consciousness their spirit/ freely given/ your flesh their body".

Burns and Smith write with a rare, pointed energy. Selwyn Pritchard's new book of radiant, fluid translations from the Chinese, *Lunar Frost* (Brandl & Schlesinger), reminds us that some traditional forms are similarly energised. Spanning the Tang (618-907) and Song (960-1279) Dynasties, *Lunar Frost* turns every moment into a year of contemplation. After reading and rereading *Lunar Frost* (it asks to be kept in a pocket, carried to where the mists rise in early morning) I must add Pritchard to my favourite translators. How gently he exposes Li Po's awareness that the world itself is lonely; how carefully assures his readers of an ancient hospitality of spirits. "One for the road, dear old friend –/ soon no one will drink your health!' writes Wang Wei. And Liu Changqing: "Dogs yelp at the gate./ Snow, our host home late." These voices sound hauntingly familiar.

Through the Letterbox: Haikus by George Bruce (Renaissance, £9.99), a collaboration between Bruce and artist Elizabeth Blackadder, edited by Lucina Prestige, first struck me as quaint. Yet, *Through the Letterbox* borders on death and this is its salvation. It asks "what's next?" and plays with the mind's inability to stop asking inane, distracting questions. We move thankfully from washy, tearoom poems such as 'For Heidi': "Dear Heidi, wind blew/ Sun shines brightly./ I am lifted up./ Thank you" to, in the beautiful haiku cycle, 'Living on the Planet', a more concentrated, contemplative approach: "What's next? Gossip. Gossip./ Say the birds. Words./ Nothing. Wait for a red moon"

The haiku never end with a full-stop – it's a question mark or nothing. I admire Blackadder's use of colour to portray a scattering of spiritual dust, drawn into the amorphous nature of her collage. But the illustrations here, save for the eloquent cover collage, are black-and-white and slightly childish, overdefined, seeking attention when the words are already speaking. This may be due to a misconception that haiku is a simple, 'black-and-white' form. In fact, it requires great attention to image as dispeller of shadows, as illuminator – both in line/line-break and, if they are to attach themselves, in pictures. I may be of a generation with no time for scrap books, but that is at times how this book feels. But the best poems are more than worth it.

In 1776, the engraver Thomas Bewick made a journey from Newcastle through the lowlands and highlands of Scotland. Sally Evans' *Bewick Walks to Scotland* (Arrowhead, £7.00) recreates this journey, in formal-sounding verse, interspersing Bewick's detailed wood engravings of skylarks, starlings, and other critters. The engravings and the poems are elegant and observational, though there is a good deal of thematic repetition. Most interesting is an attempt to escape from art, for "Our ingenuity", writes Evans in 'Lomond', "is not much use/ outside our normal flat page of etching". Brian Whittingham, in *Drink the Green Fairy* (£8.99) looks for the place where art reaches beyond its borders and caresses itself. The Green Fairy is absinthe (God bless wormwood!), and he uses Cézanne, Degas, and many more absinthe-swooners as subjects and inspiration; here constant change is cleansing. In 'The Vietnam Vet':

> He chops logs –
> dull thunking …
> The Woodsman meditates –
> like the *Sioux* before him
> who cleansed
> themselves of all human scent

Here is gentle celebration, a conscious shedding, and a steady gaze with global reach.

Travelogues, pictures and history in Tom Bryan's *Twa Tribes: Scots Among the Native Americans* (NMS, £7.99), clarify the relationship of Scots to Native Americans during European settlement in North America. Following Hugo Reid, Alexander Ross and Charles McKenzie, all of whom became intimate with native language and culture, Bryan doesn't romanticise these adventurers, nor does he crush them with political correctness. The results are illuminating and give a real taste of life in the old frontier – from tending cattle, navigating unexplored coastline to crossing cold rivers, beavers in sight.

A unique art book, *Drawing David Daiches* (Talbot Rice Gallery: £7.00), with portrait drawings by Joyce Gunn Cairns, accompanies an exhibition of the same name. The extracts aren't necessary; Cairns' portraiture does astounding work on its own. But the snippets are chosen well, spanning Professor Daiches' wide-ranging career and showcasing the extent of his hallmark, relentless, graceful tone as poet and critic, man of Edinburgh and International Letters. Inspired, perhaps, by Daiches' adage that "art is greater than its interpreters", Cairns plays with our preconceptions. The drawings look as though there are many faces at once, but when you look closely … well, you *can't* look closely, because her portraiture won't allow anything but honest, momentary being. *Try to get closer*, her drawings seem to taunt, challenging the viewer; *there is nothing closer than your own perception. Many faces in one face is the strange way of the world.*

Also struggling with perception is Alexis Lykiard's *Skeleton Keys* (Red Beck, £6.95). Lykiard writes with what Yannis Goumas calls a "true Greek directness". He highlights complex undercurrents of wartime Greece, but this "directness" can neutralise otherwise potent moments. In 'Observation': "men, women, children, of whom none/ was destined to be spared". The matter-of-fact voice is used with effect and historical urgency. In 'Diaspora, of Sorts': "due attention paid/ my long-lost mother, for just one. Among/ so many others, the dead lovers, friends". Perhaps this struggle in phrasing is part of the emotional Diaspora he amplifies, its call familiar, painful. There are shining moments, but whether compassion is summoned or sacrificed is hard to tell: in 'Mikis Theodorakis':

> such creatures as despise creation,
> envy everyone who moves
> lovingly, serenely toward myth
> without – and far beyond – them.

In fiction, two new short story collections are uncompromising and historical. John Herdman, in *Four Tales* (Zoilus, £12), writes with the laconic wit of an Elizabethan Fool. Beyond wit, his talent is for a Doestoyevsky-like methodical breakdown of society and its discontents. 'A Truth Lover' begins, "Freedom: by definition, what has not been attained." There are no still lives; Herdman illuminates the subtleties of change. In *Vivaldi and the Number 3* (Serpent's Tail, £8.99), Ron Butlin recreates, re-mosaics composers' and philosophers' lives to reveal a hybrid structure of human isolation and creation, their shifting key signatures. While Herdman's writing is solid and unbreakable, Butlin's stories are synaesthetic, gladly turning to liquid and scattering into the sky. A combined Strauss/Amenhotep IV receives emails; Hume, recalling Christ and the fish-and-bread episode, reasons that "a few loaves and fishes" have "fed Scotland for generations" ... where's the miracle? Mozart becomes a private eye, but not for long. The pages are strewn with miracles, and Butlin constantly demands of characters, "Show me the miraculous in your lives!" They cannot answer, caught between dreams of fame and transcendence, and realities of screwy political chaos. The world has become more drunk and doesn't remember drinking at all.

Two new books from bluechrome, Dee Rimbaud's *Dropping Ecstasy with the Angels* (£7.99) and William Oxley's *London Visions* (£6.99) are popular poetry – colourful, accessible. Rimbaud's words have a fractal pulse, though often lack concision. There are tender moments ("You bend to a higher will,/ Sensing the rhythm of light" in 'The Silver Light') and a New Age sense of wandering and forced wonder. Oxley searches for a London where love is "answered". King's Cross is a "cathedral of journeys" and his poems read as sermons in a religion of observation. 'Dictionary London' begins, "Who never tired of London but was often tired of life." This delightful, Londonesque paradox drives the volume.

In the realm of popular poetics, *Graffiti in Red Lipstick* (Curly Snake, £6.95) by Magi Gibson and *Bad Ass Raindrop* (£6.95) by Kokumo Rocks provide a rough and wildly feminine balance to Rimbaud and Oxley. Rare among performance poets, who can favour anger and adrenaline over insight, Kokumo Rocks (rhythm in the name alone!) urges people to step back and watch the war fighting itself, listen to its rhythms. She looks at the mechanics of the world, the insideworkings of hatred and love. In 'Windows': "Windows like sheets of ice/ You cling to the wall/ Secured by man". In 'Growing Up Black in Scotland': "I wonder if we exist at all". These are physical stories without fear. Without fear? "Be proud of what you got/ Cause baby, it's good/ And it's hot."

Graffiti in Red Lipstick begins with 'the poet', where a seemingly-still body is orbited by a wild mind, "like a buzzard, she circles/ the sky of her imagination". By the end, the mind has calmed but the body is flying forward, "sitting on this train, speeding/ forwards, thinking back ... I search my bag/ for paper, pen, find none// my hand locates a lipstick – red –/ the vinyl seats in front invite// I write ..." The voices conjured are trapped, unaware of their own darkness. As a result of captivity, they are possessed, always a sexual possession. In 'spoils of war', "you would have made a whore of her/ the twelve year old girl ... and now you would make/ a murderer of me". Does this differ from Rocks' 'Murder', which ends, "Murder murder murder/ In the first degree/ Murder!'"? Not at all. Both voices search for speech that may bring healing. There is a corrupt sexual, racial religion all around us, they preach: we need an independent state, based in story, not violence.

Bashabi Fraser's *Tartan & Turban* (Luath, £8.99) brings an Asian emphasis on suffering as transformation (rather than struggle as gain and loss). She laughs at Gods and Goddesses and speaks as an Earth-Mother when nothing else seems to work. In 'I am the ABSOLUTE':

I stand at the centre, resolute,
Unwilling to multiply or be divided
Except in your dreams of the ABSOLUTE.

She is serious and not serious; she asks in what ways dreaming forges a unity, life is an accumulation of toxins. "If faith in God divides/ The human race", she writes in 'The Great Divider', "Then let me live in doubt/ And isolation". In 'On a moonless night' her grandmother fasts "Each year before/ The cold winds blow", and she must know why, "Is it to chase the dark away/ That rules her measured sky?" Poetry is concerning itself with ritual – not as salvation or curse, but as cause and effect, as a social reality affecting assimilation, defining prejudice.

Unlike those social toxins concerning Bashabi, which stick around because we are afraid to decompose, *The Rubaiyat of Omar Khayyam* won't go away because it's too damn fun. Rab Wilson's Scots translation for Luath (£8.99) works with a storyteller's talent for understatement to emphasise the pathetic (*"There's naebody made ye play"*) and the dirty, comic social realities in every adventure: "Okay. Ye micht've slept wi a whoor or twae,/ An leeved in the fast lane aa yer life,/ When ye come tae the slip road, ye can kiss it aa goodbye/ An yer life micht as weel hae been juist a dream."

Though I don't understand the infliction of Shakespearean quotes ("To be, or not to be – ye ken whit ah mean?"), it *is* invigorating to find "penthouses" and "fast lanes" where I remembered only Lions and Lizards, in previous versions. Fitzgerald's standard translation (included here) captures both the fool and the hero, in sparking dialectic; Wilson's Scots draws the rambling alkie. This brings the self-deprecating humour needed to accept the droning message that "This place hus only got twa doors: '*In*' an '*Oot*',/ An aa it's got tae oaffir is grief and daith." Wilson's translation is distinctly intimate. It cuts away a third, personal door, not overly concerned with where that door might lead.

Roderick Watson's *Into the Blue Wavelengths: Love Poems and Elegies* (Luath, £8.99) and Dennis O'Donnell's *Smoke and Mirrors* (Curly Snake, £6.95) use upsetting techniques to reach admirable goals. Watson's language is firm and flailing, like Whirling Dervishes, but at times the rhythm lacks precise passion; many poems in standard English strain toward the grittiness and honesty of his Scots ("On account o luve at the beginning, God Himsel/ cam doon…(Or that's hoo the Faither telt it.)". Yet, this incantorial precision also brought me back in, to the sound of elegiac love in everyday language. In *Smoke and Mirrors,* many poems are there in brilliant endings, and I wondered at the initial ramblings. But they draw in images like the point of a prism sweeping in a triangle of light. This allows O'Donnell to expand outside himself, uncovering an electric compassion that reaches its zenith in 'All Done by Mirrors', set in an asylum:

> Save for the fact that no one shouts "Action!" they're veteran actors in a remake …

waiting for the big black train they remember from childhood.

In Liz Niven's *Burning Whins and Other Poems* (Luath, £8.99), there is death in eroticism, movement in stillness, and the mind moves through the world, trying to catch bits in its net. The tanka-like movement from moment to moment is sometimes rich, but more often feels didactic or self-evident, as in 'Picasso's Timeshare': "It is in the smallest of everyday matters/ we find our art". Don't tell – show! Another Luath release, Angus Calder's *Sun Behind the Castle: Edinburgh Poems* (£8.99), relishes in tenderness and focuses its lens on the invisible writing on the ancient city's walls. In 'Atmospherics', bin-bags are exposed – not what's in them (though that as well), but the animals surrounding them; the beasts they support. Calder delights in unplugging the fuel that drives situations, that hides history. In part two: "Truth is a child … Out of today into/ tomorrow with effort." Calder's much-loved update of Horace's odes, 'Horace in Tollcross', appears as well, as cunning as ever.

Bloodaxe Books never fails to impress with the stunning quicksand and cohesion of its collections. These are sensual almanacs, embodied by voices unraveling their seams. Invoking the Fool of Tarot (mortality?), she incants, "May the light land/ every day differently on your bird-table/ mackerel black/ mackerel silver". These are vigorous poems, gathering together as if creating a golem. Where is it headed? What does it desire? Conn is relentlessly serious. *Ghosts at Cockcrow* looks at the divide between what people know and what they think they want. He challenges: "the test, to this day, whether Scotland retains/ the will to grasp the thistle, not the thistledown." Hospital ghosts chill unblinkingly in 'Ministrations': Jen Hadfield's *Almanacs* (£7.95), Stewart Conn's *Ghosts at Cockcrow* and Roddy Lumsden's *Mischief Night: New and Selected Poems* (both £8.95) balance and twirl mandalas of the psyche. "The ghosts who haunt us/ … will rise ahead of us/ bearing pills and bedpans."

Hadfield's hub is archetypes and lore, her movements tidal, sharp.

Lumsden, too, speaks unspoken fears. He is one of the few worthwhile deadpan poets: "... the salt of hopelessness/ which confirms me as human" is scattered copiously throughout, with unexpected curl and bite. *Mischief Night* ranges from the annoyingly memorable *Roddy Lumsden is Dead* (*"I do not suffer for my art, I just suffer."*) to a coy feeling of revelation. In 'Against Naturism':

> ... Eve discovered modesty and slipped in and out of something comfortable ... but ours is human nature – things come off so rarely. Come in. Let me take your coat.

Christopher Whyte's bold new critical work, *Modern Scottish Poetry* (Edinburgh University Press) seeks to pull away from a nationalist agenda, from minimizing and distortion that "establish a national canon which ... risks mimicking that which it aimed to replace". Eventually he wants "Scottishness" to live and breathe, but this book is mostly an attempt at untying the ropes. Marina Tsvetayeva drives the thought process: "Writing poetry is in itself translating, from the mother tongue into another ... No language is the mother tongue. Writing poetry is rewriting it ..." Though Whyte's aim is clear: we must learn to relate to "concepts of nation ... [with a sense of] play, of imagination, invention, and paradoxical renewal and reversal" – he constantly qualifies his arguments and critical ('circular') framework and we get either edgy introduction or dizzying close readings, in dislocating flux. Particularly strong and renewing are his dealings with early Scots and Gaelic foundational work. "The purpose of criticism is to enrich the experience of reading, to send us continually back to the text". The few poets selected are so belaboured that we are sent away from the poetry considered and its criticism to look for other poets outside the summoned debate over nationcentric tendencies and the politics of poetry; perhaps his readings are *too* specific in the face of broad historical debate. Whyte intends to catalyse, and the sparks are fine-tuned and flying high.   *Ari Messer*

Theatre Roundup
Varying the theatre Tipple

The Royal Lyceum kicked off the 2005 Season with a dynamic revival of John Osborne's *Look Back in Anger*. David Tennant was a dangerous Jimmy Porter as he leapt on and off chairs and stools, treating his more privileged wife with brutal brusqueness, while Stephen McNicoll as the Welshman who helped him run a sweetie stall was a strong and essential foil to Tennant's bravado. The play stood up very well. The surroundings might be 1950s but there are parallels to the today's newly qualified graduates making-time jobs that demand little education.

Graduate Porter rails at the establishment; politicians aren't listening to him or his generation. Cliff's the dourer, lumpen young man who gets on with it, smoking his cigarettes while trying to hide his affection for Alison, he lacks the destabilising insight Porter battles with. Osborne's script was given tight, sharp direction by Richard Baron and Tennant's performance was awarded the Critics' Award for Theatre in Scotland (CATS) for Best Male Performance.

The next play was a co-production with The Bush Theatre, London, of Sharman Macdonald's *The Girl With Red Hair*. Some playwrights work in a narrow band of experience or setting: Macdonald revisits a Scottish seaside village and the characters of two eccentric older women, not the main character, who was someone we never meet – a young woman who died in a car accident. A year on, her former boyfriend, her mother and others weave in memories so the dead girl still lives in them. Unrolling slowly and undramatically failed to engage many. But if you want to be lapped gently round the themes of loss and memory, Macdonald's play was emotionally soothing and lyrical.

John Clifford's new dramatisation of Tolstoy's novel *Anna Karenina* was directed by Muriel Romanes for the Royal Lyceum. Francis O'Connor's transforming set yielded a dramatic climax recalling the Victorian love of spectacle on stage. Indeed it was hard not to fear the engine under full steam had not only crushed Anna but would hurtle off the stage and flatten the audience!

Clifford brought out both Anna's story and the emotional lives of two other couples. The gone-astray brother Oblonsky and wife Kitty drew uncomfortable laughs as Cara Kelly and Paul Blair bring to life the recognisable strains of maturing marriage. Liam Brennan (nominated for a CATS award) excelled as the awkward Levin whose halting, anguished wooing of Louise Collin's Kitty brought lumps to throats, tears to eyes and then smiles of delight and warmth. Unfortunately Raquel Cassidy's and Jamie Lee's, Anna and Vronsky didn't exude the fierce sparks that alert you to a dangerous liaison erupting. But the adaptation brought out the themes of the novel and our human flawed lives and gloried in a cast, some playing many roles, so it felt richly populated.

Another revival finished the season, Tom McGrath's *Laurel and Hardy* rejoiced in Tony Cownie's direction. Steven McNicoll's superb comic timing gave us Hardy closely matched by Barnaby Power's Laurel, with Jon Beales' on-stage live musical accompaniment. Neil Murray's film lot set bolstered the play's iconic feeling. From the opening to the close when they danced off into legend as if presaging Morecambe and Wise, the production brought out the pathos and struggle behind the scenes. Like Tolstoy's Levin, Hardy found being a creative artist far from easy. With live enactments of those moments etched in our black and white film memories, and Rita Henderson's choreography the slick engine of this revival was well tuned.

The second Season under Mark Thomson suggests an artistic director hitting his stride early. Other Scottish theatres seemed stuck in a loop of sameness which leaves audiences short changed; having two drams of the same whisky, the taste gets dimmed.

The Traverse have produced no new shows since August 2004, but fielded two in Spring 2005, both texts published by Nick Hern Books. The first was *One Day All This Will Come To Nothing* by Catherine Grosvenor, directed by Philip Howard. A young police officer, Anna, Molly Innes, (CATS nomination), with missing boyfriend, stands by the corpse of a man washed up by the sea. Elsewhere a young man tries to bury himself when a man comes and offers a new life. We move between the two men and Anna, her life and visits to her missing partner's parents, and possible storylines build up. Though individual scenes have moments, the ambition gets mired in the increasing gloom of Anna's breakdown and the confusion of who these people really were. It is a play about lost modern people and it ultimately lost itself.

The Traverse went to China and selected Wang Xiaoli's *In The Bag* for translation by Ronan O'Donnell. In China or Scotland, the vacuousness of a comfortable life where shopping, clubbing and drinking are used to fill the leisure hours, consumerism is IT. While well served by O'Donnell, director Lorne Campbell and the varying widely in experience cast, the story of two brothers, one a writer and their partners goes nowhere. This is another play from the Traverse that reflect modern 30-somethings' lives and no more. Audiences need variety – the Traverse *must* encourage writers to write something other than an identifiable Traverse play. Our writers are capable and different styles of creation *should* be explored.

Douglas Maxwell made a welcome return to productions of two plays, both published by Oberon Books. *Mancub* is a dramatisation of a little-known children's novel, *The Flight of the Cassowary* by John Levert, about Paul, a boy who thinks he can become an animal. Vanishing Point's production, finely directed by Matthew Lenton, introduced us to Paul's world, plus laconic next door dog, Paul's exasperated Dad, his teach-er and his troubled at home friend Jerry all played by the watchable Sandy Grierson as well as his Mother, possible girlfriend Karen Cleary, another dotty teacher Mr Fideles, and Jerry's traumatised-by-the-war Grandmother, played by the equally compelling Claire Lamont, all seen through Paul J Corrigan's excellent Paul. The play and production, about sanity and human life, touched deep and also gladden and excited the heart, not a combination Traverse plays seem capable of these days.

The other Maxwell play was a co-production by Dundee Rep and Paines Plough, directed by John Tiffany, *If Destroyed True*. The production using originally music and choreographed moments suggesting Tiffany's appointment at the National Theatre of Scotland as Associate Director (New Work) will add colour to next season.

Paul Thomas Hickey as the narrator Vincent, a young man born as his young mother, Cora Bisset, died and David Ireland as Ty, one of his friends joined the Rep's ensemble. Robert Patterson as town chemist, a seemingly respectable man with slime on his hands, added to his increasingly repertoire of creepy men. Vincent is a self-designated artist who decides to be creative about the project to revive New Flood, one of those neglected, grimy little ex-industrial Scottish towns. The script is strongly musical, and Hickey who was never off stage keeps us with the text during its very occasional lulls.

Maxwell gets in digs at the small pompous minds exemplified by Patterson's chemist, his uncomfortable satire reminiscent of Durrenmatt's play *The Visit*, directed by Martin Danziger in a Rep production just before Maxwell's play. It used Maurice Valancy's adaptation of Dürrenmatt's text, scripted by Peter Arnott into Scots with large performances by Gerry Mulgrew as Freddie and Ann Louise Ross as Clarrie, one-time lover of the possible saviour for the town. Unfortunately seeing these two similar plays one after the other diminished the impact of both.

Paines Plough in a co-production with the Tron premiered David Grieg's play *Pyrenees*, set in a hotel at the base of those mountains. Grieg revisits his fascination with men that disappear: here the man has lost his memory and the awkward embassy official, female and young, finds a surprising fascination in the Scottish accented stranger. Then the older woman, the wife, appears. With a glorious fourth character, the hotelier who can connect himself to all nations, this script is humorous and fun to watch. It also contains philosophical subtexts – who are we, is it stable, if not are we? Directed by Vicky Featherstone who is now the head of the National Theatre of Scotland, again this production suggests NToS should set sail well steered.

Also in Glasgow Davey Anderson, a new playwright, has been steadily developing and, as a winner of 2005 The Arches Award for Stage Directors, directed his new play *Snuff*. Billy returning from Iraq looks up his mate Kevin who's ensconced in a high-rise Glasgow flat and also hopes to see Kevin's sister Pamela. In a script which leads us closer and closer to a increasingly troubling destination Anderson weaves in Protestant bigotry, the effects on fearful minds of the media and politically-induced war of terror, and how men still need to learn to talk to each other and the opposite gender. It will be at the 2005 Fringe – a strong script from a young man revealing a theatrical soul.

New work is increasingly at the heart of the Scottish Theatre season, but serious attention should be paid to the companies working in the challenging world of children's theatre. Some start not from a script to put on its feet but a vision they want to fly and the result can have a liberating, multilayered texture that retains the life of its creation. Some words are avoided when discussing theatre in Scotland: our juvenility as a theatrical nation is revealed for 'devising' is one. The strength of the best devised work is that it is always reaching out to each audience anew. This way of working that enriches creatives brave and bright enough to try it. A true coming of age for theatre in Scotland will need to contain within it the demanding quality of theatre we mistakenly avoid because it's created by companies for under-age audiences who'd like to create for us all. After all only the unimaginative never vary their tipple.

Thelma Good

Pamphleteer

The psychoanalyst Adam Phillips described poetry as the last true art – it offers little in the way of audience, money or celebrity – literally art for art's sake. Poetry persists and nowhere is this more evident than in pamphlets. Pamphleteering continues to grow and offers fertile ground for creativity.

Shag (Arrowhead, Darlington, £4.00) is by Sue Vickerman, winner of the 2003 Biscuit Publishing Poetry Prize. Whether reflecting on family relationships or relationships in nature, these poems are as sharp and keen-eyed as the birds that scud through them. 'Waiting for Puffins' describes a fruitless expedition to see the distinctive seabirds: "But there are no bright, calypso beaks, jolly as plastic;/ no sad-eyed, comical sea-birds from book-spines/ and cartoons, the ones you promised; only auks'/ dark looks and razorbillls' blunt chins, and my eye-/ corners lapped by the encroaching edge of the sea." 'Northern Sights' tries to imagine the blunted world of someone without sight and the inadequacy felt in trying to empathise: "But your stick tap-dances over my rehearsal,/ avoiding objects, except that you say/ coffee smells the same, and I accept/ that the rush of air as you landed was universal". These poems are precisely observed miniatures, rich in detail and gently atmospheric.

From the vulnerabilities of perception to the vulnerabilities of introspection in Patricia Ace's *Intensive Care* (Ace Press, www.scottish-pamphlet-poetry.com, £4.00), which is divided between the themes of Nurture and Nature. Ace is particularly fine at crafting detail, from the raw *Intensive Care*, and its devastating depiction of a sick new-born baby: "Limp and pain-filled shell/ For me to stare at …/ Unbelieving", to the quieter musings on the girls whose names she removes from her daughter's second-hand uniform in 'Nametapes'. The 'Nature' section deals with passion and betrayal, and contains impressive sonnets which lift the overall mood. In 'Symbiosis' she adapts Elizabeth Barrett Browning's 'Let me count the ways': "Like a fish that scours the flank of a whale/ following all of its days." These poems don't interfere or proselytise but they do attempt to explain everyday, realistic fears – explanations being more satisfying than descriptions.

Casanova's 72nd Birthday is a Ravenscraig Poetry Pamphlet (Akros Publications, 33 Lady Nairn Avenue, Kirkcaldy, £3.95) by Norman Kreitman. Kreitman has produced two earlier collections and this is a selection of 29 poems from a considerable number written since 1989. This is an accomplished collection that meanders, fugue-like and sensuous, through the mind. Beautiful phrases and clipped images such as in 'Privilege': "he resented the way she dropped her clothes/ as if they were merely facts" linger in the mind.

Alex Cluness' *Disguise* (Kettillonia, 24 South Street, Newtyle, £3.00) takes up the theme of love as a latent fire that overshadows pleasure in anything else, and how we run away from it through assorted masquerades. Cluness looks to Bob Dylan for a premise: "Everybody's wearing a disguise/ To hide what they've got left behind their eyes", and looks at the masks that people wear to carry out their daily tasks. Of 'The Astronaut': "This should be amazing/ Said the astronaut/ Dangling like a piltock/ From the white line/ Of the Shuttle/ But all I can think of/ Is her/ - Bloody hell". These fluent, unpretentious poems suggest that happiness does not come from blindly following reason.

Also from Kettillonia are *Scottish Faust: Poems and ballads of eldritch Lore* by Tom Hubbard and four tales by Mary McIntosh in *The Gless Hoose* (both £3.00). Hubbard dwells on the Faust tradition, sometimes through the voice of medieval polymath Michael Scot: "All vanished. – Yet the subtleties/ Of his own soul were gleaned,/ And mixed in just such quantities/ To call up the Arch-Fiend.", and doffs his cap to Shakespeare, Berlios, R L Stevenson and others who have explored the Diabolical myth. Hubbard lures the reader through many heady referential twists and turns, is clever, well crafted and inventive. Hubbard never fails in nerve or imagination.

Far more disturbing are Mary McIntosh's short stories in Scots which concentrate on hard lives at the bottom of the heap, where selling your soul for knowledge would seem wasteful. 'Dinna Forget Alice' looks at two friends who cheer themselves up with a sunshine holiday while a third rots in a drab nursing home with dementia: "The smell o cracklin cleanness melled wi auld age and death filled her nostrils. She luikit at the picter sittin on tap of the telly. Her bein bridesmaid tae Alice. Twa fowk she didnae ken ony mair." In 'First Fit', a soldier lies dying in Bosnia havering between redemption and a last act of brutality. "It wis an auld sang o auld wars and freedom sair come by. The bairn looked up, een wide open and her tears fell ower its broo. The words thirled in the the darkness./ 'Fuck ye, fuck the lot o ye.'/ He raised the gun. It wis het atween his fingers." This disparate collection is abundant in the psychological lubricant of misery, propelling the protagonists towards extremes.

Depleted serotonin levels are boosted by Christopher Barnes' lavender-coloured *Love Bites* (Chanticleer Press, 6/1 Jamaica Mews, Edinburgh, £2.40). Drawing from *Brewer's Dictionary of Phrase and Fable* to Bosie, Jean Genet, and vampires these full-blooded poems candidly imagine homosexual experience through history. In 'Sade's Caribbean Conquest Visits Paris' we are told: "Trample my prurience on the rack./ Spike me with the vehemence of your half-heartedness./ Stagger me with thumbikins/ or the thumbscrews of the star-crossed/ holding hands." Hmm.

The Picture from Here by Tom Kelly (Sand, PO Box 1091, Sunderland, £4.00) is a collection of 36 poems about people gone or going. These start as measured, reflective utterances that spread out like tarred bronchiole to the edges of society. From a daughter leaving home, in 'The Slow Going': "Tonight, I check her room, the covers a forced-back eyelid,/ bed empty/ as my riddled heart."; to 'One Day' which depicts the income-support existence of a young couple. "They've got a place together,/ two kids,/ one to another lad./ He carries the bairn on his shoulders,/ 'One day this will be yours'/ tattooed in the sky." Kelly's inventive similes give some of the shorter poems a proverbial quality, making them succinct and satisfying.

Also in a reflective mood is Gordon Jarvie's *Room for a Rhyme from Time to Time* (Harpercroft Books, 24 Castle Street, Crail, £2.95). Many of the poems have previously appeared in *Poetry Scotland* and *The Herald* and they concentrate on change, inheritance, and the obvious pleasure that Jarvie gets from the landscape. Although the preponderance of dedicated poems may score highly on the familial clapometer, they leave the reader feeling faintly excluded.

Sticking to traditional themes and forms, Ian Caws' *The Blind Fiddler* (Pikestaff Pamphlets, Ellon House, Harpford, Sidmouth, £3.00) is his eleventh collection and takes its name from a Cornish standing stone. These are soothing pieces with an elegiac quality and rich in natural images. Veering away from the confessional school of poetry, these poems do precisely what they set out to do – reassure rather than remonstrate.

Jimmy Crighton's *A New Way with Time* (Poor Tom's Press, 89 Winchester Avenue, Leicester, £3.00) and David Lund's *The Brown Hills of Angus* (Pinkfoot Press, Balgavies, Forfar, £3.50) are posthumous publications. Crighton reflects on his experiences as a doctor and his diagnosis with cancer, while Lund sticks to his passion for mountains. Crighton is best when he uses his clinical vision – 'The Lovers' is his best – but he does lapse into sentimentality, leaving the reader feeling curiously blank. Lund was an artist and *The Brown Hills of Angus* is landscape poetry illustrated with his meticulous drawings. His artistic eye is abundant here – birds "palette-knife" across the sky – and his poems are full of colours and similes with a synaesthetic quality. Images are constantly shifting and words are effectively combined to subtly alter meaning. *Rosie Cox*

Catalogue 107

The great and good of Scottish literature and publishing combine in the *30th Anniversary of the Scottish Publishers Association: A Celebration* (SPA, £25/ £10) The tome is a storehouse of reminiscences, from the early days of small publishers and an even smaller HQ, through many book-fairs and oceans of booze, to the relatively sunlit uplands of today. The book reminds us of the sterling work done by the SPA in promoting Scottish publishing to the world. However, by focusing on the past, there is little attention paid to the future. Judy Moir, one of the SPA's early staff: "Where are the brave, new, grass-roots publishers who are Scotland's future?" The sad truth is that the conditions for Scottish publishers are much more repressive now. Whereas they suffered before from neglect, now publishers must survive in an unequal marketplace that favours the big guns. Anyone starting up now is guaranteed heartache.

With wide-ranging themes from Ian Hamilton Finlay to the Battle of Crete, *Disasters and Heroes: On War, Memory and Representation* (University of Wales, £16.99) is another string to Angus Calder's bow. Or, more accurately, it's a combination of threads to make up a rope since this is a collection of articles, reviews and miscelleneous offcuts mulling on war and how we remember it. The eye-catching cover of gun crew in drag aside, it's a thoughtful and learned collection with the essay on the evacuation from Crete being a real highlight. Calder's lightness of touch and wryness of tone means everything in here is never less than very well done. Parts of the book do come together, like the pieces on ordinary British experience in 1945 and New Zealand women in World War II. However, as with such collections of articles, it doesn't quite cohere.

Although long-retired, Paul Henderson Scott shows no sign of slowing down with *Scotland Resurgent* (Saltire Society, £9.99) being the latest in a long line of publications. This is also a collection of essays, reviews etc but hangs together better, partly because Scott is such an accomplished generalist – his pencil sketch of the Scottish Enlightenment boils the movement down into a digestible form. His commanding grasp of argument, passion and clear-sighting learning makes for an engaging and thoughtful volume. A start, but by no means an end, to reading Scottish history and independence.

In *Voyageurs* (Canongate, £9.99) Margaret Elphinstone claims she is merely the 'editor' of old papers. It's a nonsense of course, but one that can work. It does here, partly for the slightly obscure setting (18th century Canada) as well as Elphinstone's sure touch. A Quaker lad from the Lake District ventures out to the American Great Lakes – a frontier place – to look for his disgraced sister who has completely disappeared. On his search he gets mixed up with 'voyageurs' – fur traders travelling long distances – and the War of 1812, a forgotten spat between the US and Britain. The book looks and feels very 'literary', but is none the worse for it. It's good to see widescreen treatment for a Scottish novel, even if the 'voice' of the boy sounds a bit too modern. Expect to see Orlando Bloom playing him in the movie.

Another voyager is Kenneth White, whose *The Wanderer and his Charts* (Polygon, £9.99) is keen to get off the 'Motorway of Western Civilisation' into the backwoods of thought to start the idea of 'culture' anew. White's term for it is 'geopoetics' – using a freeform mixture of geography, ethnology, history and many other disciplines to create a way of thinking totally his own. It's an attractive idea, and makes for an invigorating read – his essay on Montaigne, for example. However, White's ego throws a substantial shadow over the work so it comes closer to a memoir than it should. If you skip over the 'I's, though, there's a lot to learn here.

Rather be a prostitute than an academic? One (anonymous) female academic would, and thinks "calling academics 'whores' is a denigration of whoring". Radical stuff, but par for the course in *Collective Action: A Bad Subjects Anthology* (Pluto, £14.99). Culled from *Bad Subjects*, a leading online political journal, the tone here is serious, but with the emphasis on quick, vigorous analysis. As such, the pieces are usually only a few pages in length – with a pungent view or rigorous analysis rattled off before moving on to the next one. Editors Megan Shaw Prelinger and Joel Schalit have just about made sure that the rigour of the articles outweighs any accusations of flippancy – the chilling piece on prison architecture being a case in point.

Eleanor Bell's *Questioning Scotland* (Palgrave, £45.00) is a no-nonsense hike through the Scotland(s) of the mind. Swiftly knocking the idea of Scottish writers obsessing about Scottishness, she argues for a move toward writers that are merely Scottish in location. Although the gallons of academese sprayed at the topic don't aid understanding, there are nuggets of insight and learning here.

As Bell is keen to point out, one of the big problems with the 'Scottish Literary Renaissance' is that it seems to have been a boys'-only club, – an unruly scout troop. Which is why *Modern Scottish Poetry* (Canongate, £20.00/ £12.99) is needed: to point out women poets, and to show they often got there before the men. Editors Dorothy McMillan and Michel Byrne's definition of 'modern' is a tad contentious but there is much to absorb here. The themes are various: mothers remembering sons (Euphemia MacDonald, Anne Stevenson), letters (Elise McKay, Val Warner), and even Girton College, Cambridge (Olive Fraser and Veronica Forrest-Thomson). Thanks to Byrne, Gaelic gets a good outing, but you feel that women are an awfully *serious* lot. There's too few poems like Rhoda Bulter's mischievous 'A Letter ta da Minister's Wife'. Note for future women's anthologies: up the fun!

Neil Munro continues to fascinate: both in Lesley Lendrum's biography and the republication of *Children of Tempest* (both House of Lochar, £22.00 and £8.39). As one of Munro's grandchildren, Lendrum has a unique insight into the life of the great Inverarian and tells his story with warmth and affection. Anyone hoping for new scandals will be disappointed: Munro's life mostly involved writing and general hackwork with a contented home life. The old rumour about Munro's pa being of the House of Argyll is aired, but the real story is engaging and fascinating – a writer realising both Para Handy and 'serious stuff' easily coexisted. A reading of the deeply atmospheric and windswept *Children of Tempest* reminds the reader of Munro's great love of his Gaelic heritage. What could he have written in Gaelic, had the environment been better suited to it?

Geology is much-neglected, probably because a lot of rock, moving very slowly, may not seem that exciting. Two books give the lie to this: *Murchison's Wanderings in Russia* (British Geological Survey, £40.00) and *The Scenery of Scotland: The Structure Beneath* (NMS, £4.99) show how the studies of Scottish geologists and the geology of Scotland can be fascinating. Although not many outside the geology community have heard of Robert Murchison, he was a giant of the field in the early 19th century, establishing the idea that the same kind of rocks might not only be spread over different landmasses, but also interlinked. The book details his journeys and findings in Russia, and although the reader does have to be a bit of a geology nut to carry on, for those who stick with it there are many insights on geology, as well as a portrait of rural Russia in passing. *The Scenery of Scotland* is easier for the lay reader to pick up and enjoy since it has pictures of Scotland's native geology, combined with clear explanations of how what got where when. Impress friends, family and nervous strangers with your knowledge that the Black Cuillins in Skye are a wonderful example of Tertiary igneous formation …

Most people's knowledge of Eskimos begins with igloos and ends with travelling in kayaks. But R Bonnerjea's *Eskimos in Europe* (BIRÓ Family, £15.00) shows this to be only the tip of the iceberg (sorry) of a deeply complex and misunderstood people. Whether a curiosity for Europeans or guides for polar explorers, Eskimos have not done well from their association with 'white men'. Bonnerjea is a firm fan of the Eskimos, treating them with respect and compassion. Although the book occasionally wears its research too much on its sleeve, this should act as a spur for other studies. A beginning, not an end, to the Eskimo's story.

A fistful of poetry books: Ágnes Nemes Nagy's *The Night of Akhenaton* (£8.95) is another edition from Bloodaxe, featuring one of Hungary's major modern poets. Translator George Szirtes are to be congratulated on bringing her to a wider audience. Ringing with Hungary's past, the title work has the eponymous Pharaoh wandering through the Hungarian Uprising of 1956. Beautiful, unique and totally engrossing.

Readers may run from William Dunbar's *Selected Poems* (Fyfield Books, £8.95). Scots is a cussed, difficult bugger at the best of times: in medieval form it's near-impossible even with a glossary. But for those with lateral reading skills, the rewards are worth it. Dunbar is not so much 'modern', as MacDiarmid has described him, but of an age but no age at all. 'Of Discretioun in Taking' is an object-lesson for tax collectors, and 'Quhat is this Lyfe' proves that some subjects remain stubbornly enigmatic: "Quhat is this lyfe bot ane straucht way to deid". What, indeed.

Alison Brackenbury reflects on life and schooldays in *Bricks and Ballads* (Carcanet, £7.95). While mulling over old science lessions is not exactly original, there is spareness and sublety here. 'Behind Lansdown Crescent' and 'Green Finch' are object-lessons in rhythm and how to create an entire atmosphere in few words. The 'Hatherley Lane School 1878-2001' sequence is less about school, more about the passing of time, the destruction/ construction of landscapes and memory. Sad, wonderful, inspiring, uneven but well worth a few shekels.

Alessandro Gallenzi mixes mischief and morality to surprisingly good effect in *A Modern Bestiary – Ars Poetastrica* (Herla, $16.00). Cats are cruel, worms are meaningless and humanity, well, less said the better. The *Ars Poetastrica* part is an impassioned epic against modern poetry (it reads better than it sounds): "May this unworthy age be smashed and burned/ … its last stupidities thrown on a midden". Amen to that.

Two quick mentions: *Scottish Surnames* (Mercat, £8.99) by David Dorward and [Charles] *MacLean's Miscellany of Whisky* (Little Press, £10.00). Dorward's book is the latest edition of the popular volume, valued by genealogists everywhere. If you've always wondered about the origins of names like Farquharson, Primrose and Scroggie (and who hasn't?), you'll find the info here. A wealth of facts also festoon Charles MacLean's volume – from the economics of whisky to the respective benefits of screwcaps and corks. Best enjoyed with a glass of 15-year-old Bruichladdich.

You could hardly accuse Queens University Press of being quiet: set up in 1999 to explore language in Ireland, they've produced a dozen volumes since. All academic in tone, and a useful research tool, the books enlighten on subjects as various as *New Studies in Scots and Gaelic*, *Language and Law in Northern Ireland* and *Travellers and their Language* (£12.50 to £19.50). Two thumbs up for really getting off the beaten path!

Apologies to the following for unseemly brevity: *TLC: The Low Countries, Volume 12* (Stichting Ons Erfdeel, £30.00/ $45.00) collects essays, artworks and other miscellena from Holland and Belgium. Lavishly done, it's an excellent, diverse, if slightly oddball showcase, as most Dutch and Belgians are. John Cairney's *The Quest for Charles Rennie Mackintosh* (Luath, £16.99) is an engaging, if conventional read, worth it for the chapter on the Willow Tea Rooms and School of Art Extension alone. Andy Hall's *A Sense of Belonging to Scotland* (Mercat, £14.99) is a photographic greatest hits of Scotland from Glencoe to Grangemouth. All good stuff – which can't be said for the clanky comments by the 'Scottish personalities' which accompany the photies.   *Edmund O'Connor*

Notes on Contributors

Shanta Acharya: Born and educated in India. Oxford scholarship 1979 for doctoral study. Visiting Scholar at Harvard 1983-85. Lives London. Website: www.shantaacharya.com.

Ruth Atkinson: lives in Perthshire and started writing short stories to help her get through the winter. This is her first published story.

Gavin Bowd: Author of three poetry collections, *Technique, Camouflage* and *Hibernaculum*, and essays and short fiction. Tanslator of Michel Houellebecq's novel, *The Possibility of an Island*.

Paul Brownsey: Once journalist, now lectures in philosophy at Glasgow University. Stories in magazines &c. Shortlisted in The Macallan 2002.

Barbara Cormack: (1938–2004) Grew up in the USA, graduated BA, married a Scot and moved to England, taking up mental health support management. Barbara was a poet all her life, but only agreed to publication just before her death.

Thelma Good: Theatre Editor of top rank Writes and lectures on theatre. Published and broadcaster writer, fascinated by our evolving culture and creators now, and by what has gone before.

Rody Gorman: Lives Isle of Skye. New Gaelic collections: *Taaaaaaadhaaaaaaa!* (diehard); *Zonda? Khamsin? Sharaav? Camanchaca?* (Leabhraichean Beaga) and *Chernilo* (Coisceim).

George Hardie: Born Hamilton 1933. Ane o the foundin editors o *Chapman*. Bides in Ingland scrieves in Scots 'the language o the hairt' and is a lifelang supporter o Hamilton Academical FC. Clearly in need o treatment.

Stuart Kelly: Poet and writer for Scotland on Sunday. His first book. *The Book of Lost Books* was describew by Muriel Spark as "fascinating". He lives in Edinburgh with wife, Sam.

Roy Kesey: stories in *McSweeney's, Georgia Review* and *Prism International* &c. Spends evenings suffering plastic-bowling-pin-related injuries at the hands of his toddlers.

Lee Kofman: Writes in Hebrew and English; author of three fiction books; lived in Russia and Israel, now in Australia; in receipt of an Australian Council Literature Board grant, and tries to understand what the hell Aussie means…

John Law: Citizen of the Scottish republic, general mover and shaker, editor of *Lallans* magazine, writes mainly for his desk drawer, from which a few items occasionally escape.

Alexis Lykiard: Recent books: the memoir, *Jean Rhys Revisited; Selected Poems* 1956-96; *Skeleton Keys* (poetry); and two translations of novels: *Heliogabalus* (Artaud), & *The Nun* (Péret).

Carl MacDougall: Presenter BBC's *Writing Scotland* and of the forthcoming *Scots Road Trip* and a four-part series, *Scots: Language of the People*. Author of many books and anthologies.

Carol McKay: Tutor on Open University's short course 'Start Writing Fiction'. Born on a utility bed in the livin room of a flat in Drumchapel, Xmas Day 1955. Lives in suburban Hamilton.

Donal McLaughlin: The first-ever Scottish Writing Fellow in Berne. Switzerland, 2004. His Scottish issue of *Sampark* (India) & Latvian edition of *Edinburgh Review* are due early 2005

Ari Messer: writer and musician. Lives in San Francisco where he composes soundscores for modern dance. Studied at Stanford and Uni Edinburgh. Ex-*Chapman* volunteer.

Edwin Morgan: Born Glasgow 1920. Appointed National Poet for Scotland 2004. Recent books: *Cathures* (2002), *Love and a Life* (2003) and *Tales from Baron Munchausen* (2004).

Eabhan Ní Shuileabháin: Poet and editor of and in many mags and books. Currently poetry editor of Dublin's Literary Magazine, *The Stinging Fly*. She is happy to let her poetry speak for her.

Dennis O'Donnell: Born and lives in West Lothian. Schoolteacher and *Scotsman* columnist, now psychiatric nurse. Books: *Two Clocks Ticking* (Saltire winner) and *Smoke & Mirror*.

Stephen Sharp: Diagnosed 1984 Paranoid Schizophrenic. Told by God to kill prostitutes and set off the fire-alarm in the Houses of Parliament. For this he was sectioned. Writing was diagnosed as a symptom of mental illness.

Eleanor Thomson: After a long love affair with Glasgow (and one special Glaswegian), decided to move to the vineyards of rural France but Glasgow will always remain her *Ville Éternelle*.

Louise Welsh: For many years Louise has made her living as a dealer in out-of-print and second-hand books. Author of *The Cutting Room* and *Tamburlaine Must Die*. Lives in Glasgow.

Rab Wilson: Bides Sanquhar, Dumfriesshire. Screives maistly in Scots and his wark appears in *Lallans* and *The Herald*. An ardent uphauder o the Scots leid he'll hijack ocht he thinks worthie, an owerset it in 'the dear auld lallans'!